QUIZ BOOK II

JUNIOR

QUIZ BOOK II

B🌾XTREE

First published 2002 by Boxtree
an imprint of Pan Macmillan Ltd
Pan Macmillan, 20 New Wharf Road, London N1 9RR
Basingstoke and Oxford
Associated companies throughout the world
www.panmacmillan.com

ISBN 0 7522 6538 5

Produced under license from Celador International Limited
Copyright © 2002 Celador International Limited

Special thanks to Katherine Arbuthnott, Don Christopher,
John Eastaff, Sally Nobbs, Matthew Speller,
Adrian Woolfe and the Question Team.

1 3 5 7 9 8 6 4 2

A CIP catalogue record for this book is
available from the British Library.

Designed and typeset by seagulls
Printed and bound by Mackays of Chatham plc, Kent

CONTENTS

How to play

A brand new quiz book designed exclusively for all you junior *Who Wants To Be A Millionaire?* fans. All those hours spent playing the first *Who Wants To Be A Millionaire? Junior* are about to pay off. Are you ready for the new challenge that could win you £1,000,000? Whether you play on your own or compete with your friends, remember to use your Lifelines wisely, and good luck!

FOR 1 PLAYER

As on *Who Wants To Be A Millionaire?*, the aim of the game is to reach £1,000,000. But before you can even go on to play the game, you must first correctly answer a question from the Fastest Finger First section. You have just 30 seconds to put the letters in the correct order. When the time's up, follow the page reference at the bottom of the page to find out if you can take your place in the hotseat and begin your climb for the cash!

Once in the hotseat

Start with a question worth £100 and once you have decided on your final answer (and you're absolutely sure...) follow the page reference at the bottom of the page to find out if you're right. If your answer is correct, you can play to win £200 and start making your way up that famous Money Tree. The page where each money level begins is listed in the answer section.

As on the programme you have three Lifelines to help you on your way to £1,000,000. You don't *have* to use them, but remember, each Lifeline can only be used once, so don't use them if you don't need to.

Fifty-Fifty

This option takes away two incorrect answers leaving the correct answer and the one remaining incorrect answer. The page reference at the bottom of each page will tell you where to look for the remaining answers.

Phone-A-Friend

If you have a telephone to hand (and a brainy friend!) ring him/her up to help you out. You have 30 seconds (and no cheating please...) to read the question to your friend and for them to tell you what they think the answer is. If there's someone else around, ask them to time your call for you.

Remember, always ask permission before you use the phone.

Ask The Audience

This works in exactly the same way as on *Who Wants To Be A Millionaire?* except we've already asked the audience so you don't have to! Simply follow the page reference at the bottom of each page to find out what our audience thought. But in the end, the decision is yours.

If you answer incorrectly at any time, you are out of the game. £1,000 and £32,000 are 'safe havens', but if you answer a question incorrectly and you have not reached £1,000 then not only are you out of the game but you will leave without a penny! If you have reached one (or both) of these havens and you answer a question incorrectly, then, depending on the stage you have reached in the game, you will leave with either £1,000 or £32,000. For example, if you are clever enough to get to £250,000, but you answer the question incorrectly, then I'm afraid you will leave with only £32,000. If at any point during the game you are unsure of an answer and don't want to risk being out of the game, you can 'stick' at the amount you have won so far and that will be your final score. As you play, use the score sheets at the back of the book to keep a running record of the amount you have won and the Lifelines you have used.

FOR 2–5 PLAYERS

Players should take it in turns at being 'Chris Tarrant' and posing questions to the other contestants. The rules are the same as for a single player (see pages 6–7). If someone reaches £1,000,000 that person is the winner and the game is over. Otherwise, once everyone else is out, the person who has won the most money is the winner.

Are you ready to play? Good. With all that money at stake, we're sure we don't need to tell you to think very carefully before you give your final answer. Good luck and be sure to remember at all times the motto for *Who Wants To Be A Millionaire?* – it's only easy if you know the answer!

FASTEST FINGER FIRST

FASTEST FINGER FIRST

1

Starting with the earliest, put these days of the week in the order they occur.

- A: Wednesday
- B: Friday
- C: Sunday
- D: Saturday

2

Starting with the earliest, put these dates in order.

- A: 1743
- B: 1703
- C: 1783
- D: 1753

3

Starting with the first, put these coats of paint in the order they would be applied.

- A: First coat of gloss
- B: Undercoat
- C: Primer
- D: Second coat of gloss

4

Put these Spice Girls in alphabetical order.

- A: Posh Spice
- B: Sporty Spice
- C: Baby Spice
- D: Scary Spice

5

Starting at 2001, put these winners of the FA cup in reverse order.

- A: Arsenal
- B: Liverpool
- C: Manchester United
- D: Chelsea

Answers on page 265

FASTEST FINGER FIRST

6

Starting with the smallest, put these pets in order of average adult size.

A: Cat

B: Pony

C: Mouse

D: Dog

7

Put these words in order to complete the title of this book: Harry Potter and...

A: Goblet

B: The

C: Fire

D: Of

8

Starting with the least, put these in order of number of wheels.

A: Unicycle

B: Quad bike

C: Tricycle

D: Bicycle

9

Put these drinks in alphabetical order.

A: Orange

B: Cola

C: Water

D: Lemonade

10

Starting with the largest, put these decimal numbers in reverse order.

A: 0.13

B: 0.98

C: 0.35

D: 0.76

? Answers on page 265

FASTEST FINGER FIRST

11

Starting with the largest, put these vegetables in order of average size.

A: Swede
B: Pea
C: Pumpkin
D: Onion

12

Starting at Middle C, put these musical notes in ascending order.

A: B
B: G
C: A
D: F

13

Put these girls' names in alphabetical order.

A: Zoe
B: Sophie
C: Chloe
D: Carol

14

Starting with the shortest, put these British wild plants in order of average height.

A: Violet
B: Daffodil
C: Primrose
D: Foxglove

15

Put these winter sports in alphabetical order.

A: Skiing
B: Snowboarding
C: Skating
D: Tobogganing

? Answers on page 265

FASTEST FINGER FIRST

16

Starting with the first of the day, put these meals in the order they would be eaten.

- A: Dinner
- B: Breakfast
- C: Tea
- D: Lunch

17

Starting with the largest, put these characters from 'Winnie-the-Pooh' in order of size.

- A: Eeyore
- B: Christopher Robin
- C: Pooh
- D: Roo

18

Put these words in order to form the title of a Disney film.

- A: New
- B: Emperor's
- C: The
- D: Groove

19

Starting with the smallest, put these French numbers in order of size.

- A: Trois
- B: Un
- C: Quatre
- D: Deux

20

Starting with the highest, put these homes in order.

- A: Basement flat
- B: Penthouse apartment
- C: House
- D: Bungalow

? Answers on page 265

FASTEST FINGER FIRST

21

Put these pantomines in alphabetical order.

A: Puss in Boots

B: Cinderella

C: Snow White

D: Babes in the Wood

22

Starting with the first, put these courses
in the order they would be eaten in a restaurant.

A: Starter

B: Pudding

C: Coffee

D: Main

23

Starting with the highest value, put this money in order.

A: 2 x 50 pence

B: 6 x 20 pence

C: 10 x 2 pence

D: 30 x 1 pence

24

Starting with the smallest,
put these in order of thickness.

A: Rope

B: Thread

C: String

D: Cable

25

Put these notes in ascending order,
according to the sol-fa scale.

A: Re

B: Do

C: Fa

D: Mi

Answers on page 265

FASTEST FINGER FIRST

26

Starting with the most, put these sports in order of number of players in the traditional games.

- A: Tennis
- B: Netball
- C: Rugby Union
- D: Hockey

27

Starting with the earliest in the year, put these months in the order they occur.

- A: October
- B: December
- C: April
- D: May

28

Starting with the lowest value, put these Scrabble tiles in order.

- A: Z
- B: E
- C: P
- D: X

29

Starting with the earliest, put these Disney cartoons in the order in which they were released.

- A: Snow White and the Seven Dwarfs
- B: The Lion King
- C: Atlantis – The Lost Empire
- D: Jungle Book

30

Put these boys' names in alphabetical order.

- A: Harry
- B: Bobby
- C: Sammy
- D: Tommy

? Answers on page 265

FASTEST FINGER FIRST

31

Starting with the largest, put the answers to these multiplications in order.

- A: 11 x 8
- B: 7 x 3
- C: 9 x 9
- D: 5 x 6

32

Starting with the youngest, put these characters from 'The Simpsons' in order of age.

- A: Homer
- B: Bart
- C: Maggie
- D: Lisa

33

Put these materials in alphabetical order.

- A: Denim
- B: Silk
- C: Wool
- D: Cotton

34

Starting with the highest in value, put these playing cards in their traditional order.

- A: Jack
- B: 10
- C: Queen
- D: King

35

Starting below the ground, put these parts of a tree in ascending order.

- A: Trunk
- B: Branch
- C: Root
- D: Leaf

Answers on page 265

FASTEST FINGER FIRST

36

Put these punctuation marks in alphabetical order.

- A: Comma
- B: Bracket
- C: Apostrophe
- D: Full stop

37

Starting with the smallest, put these creatures in order of average adult wing size.

- A: Common blue butterfly
- B: Ladybird
- C: Robin
- D: Golden eagle

38

Put the following in order, to give the title of a 1982 book by Roald Dahl.

page 17

- A: G
- B: F
- C: The
- D: B

39

Starting at the top, put these parts of the human body in order.

- A: Heart
- B: Brain
- C: Knee
- D: Stomach

40

Starting with the shortest, put these periods of time in order.

- A: Decade
- B: Millennium
- C: Year
- D: Century

? Answers on page 265

FASTEST FINGER FIRST

41

Starting with the longest, put these question words in order of length.

A: Wherefore   B: Who

C: Which   D: When

42

Put these continents in alphabetical order.

A: Africa   B: Asia

C: Antarctica   D: Australia

43

Starting with the shortest, put these in order of length.

A: Metre   B: Millimetre

C: Kilometre   D: Centimetre

44

Starting with the first, put these characters from the 'Wizard of Oz' in the order they are introduced.

A: Lion   B: Tin Man

C: Dorothy   D: Scarecrow

45

Starting with the greatest, put these shapes in order of number of sides.

A: Triangle   B: Circle

C: Pentagon   D: Square

Answers on page 265

FASTEST FINGER FIRST

46

Put these 'Mr Men' in alphabetical order.

- A: Mr Tickle
- B: Mr Bump
- C: Mr Happy
- D: Mr Greedy

47

Starting with the first, put the characters from 'The Owl and the Pussy cat' in the order they are introduced.

- A: Piggy-wig
- B: Pussy cat
- C: Owl
- D: Turkey

48

Starting at the finger tips and moving towards the body, put these parts of the arm in order.

- A: Wrist
- B: Shoulder
- C: Elbow
- D: Knuckles

49

Put these rooms in the house in alphabetical order.

- A: Attic
- B: Study
- C: Kitchen
- D: Sitting room

50

Starting with the longest, put these races in order of length.

- A: 1 mile
- B: 200 metres
- C: 800 metres
- D: Marathon

Answers on page 265

FASTEST FINGER FIRST

51

Starting with the first day of Christmas, put these gifts in the order they are given in the song.

◆A: Partridge   ◆B: French hens

◆C: Turtle doves   ◆D: Colly birds

52

Starting with the first, put these items of clothing in the order they would be put on.

◆A: Overcoat   ◆B: Vest

◆C: Jacket   ◆D: Shirt

53

Put these popstars in alphabetical order by first name.

◆A: Madonna   ◆B: Elvis Presley

◆C: Cher   ◆D: Robbie Williams

54

Starting with the largest, put these mammals in order of average adult size.

◆A: Polar bear   ◆B: Chimpanzee

◆C: Elephant   ◆D: Blue whale

55

Starting with the closest, put these UK cities in order of proximity to London.

◆A: Birmingham   ◆B: Cambridge

◆C: Glasgow   ◆D: Cardiff

? Answers on page 265

FASTEST FINGER FIRST

56

Put these letters in the order they might appear on an invitation when a reply is required.

A: S

B: P

C: V

D: R

57

Starting with the first, put these stages in a butterfly's life cycle in order.

A: Chrysalis

B: Egg

C: Adult

D: Caterpillar

58

Starting with the least number of letters, put these capital cities in order.

A: Paris

B: London

C: Rome

D: Washington

59

Starting with the smallest, put these UK coins in order of size.

A: 5 pence

B: 2 pound

C: 20 pence

D: 50 pence

60

Put these words in order to form the title of a children's TV series.

A: Witch

B: Teenage

C: The

D: Sabrina

Answers on page 265

FASTEST FINGER FIRST

61

Starting with the largest, put these birds in order of size.

A: Wren   B: Ostrich
C: Golden eagle D: Blackbird

62

Starting with the earliest, put these Queens of England in order of their accession to the British throne.

A: Victoria   B: Elizabeth II
C: Elizabeth I   D: Mary I

63

Starting with the longest, put these words in order of number of letters.

A: Literature   B: Language
C: Mathematics   D: Geography

64

Put these gardening tasks in alphabetical order.

A: Digging   B: Hoeing
C: Pruning   D: Planting

65

Starting with the earliest, put these times of day in the order they occur.

A: Midday   B: 0700
C: Midnight   D: 1500

Answers on page 265

FASTEST FINGER FIRST

66

Starting with the nearest to London,
put these counties in order.

A: Cornwall
B: Hampshire
C: Devon
D: Surrey

67

Starting with the least, put these words
in order of the number of vowels.

A: Able
B: Above
C: Apt
D: Abundance

68

Put these words in order to complete the rhyme,
'Tinker, Tailor, Soldier, Sailor'.

A: Beggarman
B: Poor man
C: Rich man
D: Thief

page
23

69

Starting with the largest, put these
sea creatures in order of size.

A: Sardine
B: Whale
C: Salmon
D: Shark

70

Starting with the closest, put these countries
in order of distance from London.

A: USA
B: Australia
C: France
D: Spain

FASTEST FINGER FIRST

71

Put these TV shows in the order they first appeared.

A: Who wants to be a Millionaire?
B: Blockbusters
C: University Challenge
D: Fifteen to One

72

Starting with the earliest, put these inventions in the order they appeared.

A: Television
B: Radio
C: Telephone
D: Walkman

73

Put these words in order to form the title of a famous film.

A: Music
B: The
C: Of
D: Sound

74

Starting with the smallest, put these musical instruments in order of size.

A: Cello
B: Double bass
C: Violin
D: Triangle

75

Put these words in order to form the title of a song by Westlife.

A: Man
B: Makes
C: What
D: A

 Answers on page 265

FASTEST FINGER FIRST

76

Starting at the front, put these parts of a car in order.

A: Front bumper   B: Bonnet
C: Boot   D: Steering Wheel

77

Starting with the most recent,
put these Royals in order of birth.

A: The Queen   B: Queen Mother
C: Prince Charles   D: Prince Harry

78

Starting with the first in the year, put these
annual events in the order in which they occur.

A: Boxing Day   B: Christmas Day
C: Bonfire Night   D: Halloween

79

Put these oceans in alphabetical order.

A: Indian   B: Atlantic
C: Pacific   D: Arctic

80

Starting with the earliest, put these
wives of Henry VIII in order.

A: Catherine Parr   B: Catherine of Aragon
C: Anne Boleyn   D: Jane Seymour

? Answers on page 265

FASTEST FINGER FIRST

81

Starting with the largest, put these angles in order of size.

A: Right angle

B: Acute angle

C: Obtuse angle

D: Reflex angle

82

Starting with the first, put these Gospels in the order they appear in the Bible.

A: Luke

B: Matthew

C: John

D: Mark

83

Starting with the smallest, put these Roman numerals in order of size.

A: III

B: V

C: X

D: I

84

Put these words in order to form the title of a play by Shakespeare.

A: Night's

B: Dream

C: A

D: Midsummer

85

Starting with the smallest, put these items of crockery in order of size.

A: Side plate

B: Saucer

C: Dinner plate

D: Platter

? Answers on page 265

FASTEST FINGER FIRST

86

Starting with the largest, put these parts of the human body in average adult size.

- A: Hand
- B: Foot
- C: Finger
- D: Toe

87

Starting with the largest, put these modes of transport in order of average size.

- A: Taxi
- B: Bus
- C: Tricycle
- D: Train

88

Put these British monarchs in the order they reigned.

- A: George IV
- B: George III
- C: George I
- D: George II

89

Starting with the smallest, put these spoons in order of average size.

- A: Teaspoon
- B: Tablespoon
- C: Salt spoon
- D: Dessert spoon

90

Starting with the youngest, put these relations in order of age.

- A: Mother
- B: Sister
- C: Great grandmother
- D: Grandmother

Answers on page 265

FASTEST FINGER FIRST

91

Put these rivers in alphabetical order.

◆A: Nile ◆B: Thames

◆C: Amazon ◆D: Seine

92

Starting at the lowest level, put these in order.

◆A: Beach ◆B: Mountain

◆C: Hill ◆D: Sea floor

93

Starting with the youngest, put these film classifications in order of ascending age admission.

◆A: 15 ◆B: PG

◆C: 12 ◆D: U

94

Put these words in order to form the title of a book by E Nesbit.

◆A: And ◆B: Children

◆C: It ◆D: Five

95

Put these words in order to complete this title of a Britney Spears UK No 1 hit: 'Oops! ...'

◆A: Did ◆B: I

◆C: Again ◆D: It

Answers on page 265

FASTEST FINGER FIRST

96

Starting with the least, put these words in order of how many times the letter S appears in each.

A: Sessions

B: Essay

C: Pains

D: Seashells

97

Put these tennis stars in alphabetical order by first name.

A: Venus Williams

B: Serena Williams

C: Tim Henman

D: Greg Rusedski

98

Starting at the top, put these parts of a boat in order.

A: Deck

B: Crow's nest

C: Wheelhouse

D: Rudder

99

Starting with the smallest, put these pieces of rock in order of size.

A: Boulder

B: Pebble

C: Sand

D: Stone

100

Starting at 'GO' on a standard British Monopoly board, put these stations in the order they would be passed.

A: Kings Cross

B: Marylebone

C: Fenchurch Street

D: Liverpool Street

Answers on page 265

50:50		

15 **£1 MILLION**

14 £500,000

13 £250,000

12 £125,000

11 £64,000

10 **£32,000**

9 £16,000

8 £8,000

7 £4,000

6 £2,000

5 **£1,000**

4 £500

3 £300

2 £200

1 ◆ £100

page
31

1

Which of the following is not a tree?

- A: Oak
- B: Ash
- C: Willow
- D: Snowdrop

2

The author Lewis Carroll was famous for writing which of these books?

- A: Heidi's Adventures in Wonderland
- B: Mary's Adventures in Wonderland
- C: Jane's Adventures in Wonderland
- D: Alice's Adventures in Wonderland

3

Which animal lives in a stable?

- A: Horse
- B: Sheep
- C: Cow
- D: Pig

4

What is a junior Girl Guide known as?

- A: Brownie
- B: Bluey
- C: Greenie
- D: Reddie

5

Which household machine sucks up dust and dirt from floors and carpets?

- A: Microwave
- B: Spin-dryer
- C: Vacuum cleaner
- D: Food mixer

50:50 Go to page 241   Go to page 253   **?** Answers on page 265

1 ◆ £100

6

How is the non-working period between Friday evening and Sunday evening known?

- A: Fortnight
- B: Weekend
- C: End of the month
- D: Holiday

7

Which of these is not red?

- A: Tomato
- B: Cherry
- C: Banana
- D: Strawberry

8

What accompanies 'noughts' to make a well known game?

- A: Circles
- B: Crosses
- C: Diamonds
- D: Squares

page 33

9

Which meal is usually the first of the day?

- A: Dinner
- B: Breakfast
- C: Lunch
- D: Supper

10

Wool is sheared from which animals?

- A: Sheep
- B: Cows
- C: Dogs
- D: Cats

50:50 Go to page 241   Go to page 253   Answers on page 265

11

Which of these is a popular card game?

A: Snap
B: Crackle
C: Pop
D: Wallop

12

What is put into fountain pens?

A: Tea
B: Lemonade
C: Ink
D: Water

13

Which of these is a tool for washing and wiping floors?

A: Bop
B: Hop
C: Fop
D: Mop

14

What is the part of the day between sunrise and midday?

A: Morning
B: Afternoon
C: Evening
D: Night

15

Which food can be boiled, roasted, mashed or chipped?

A: Potato
B: Spaghetti
C: Rice
D: Cabbage

50:50 Go to page 241  Go to page 253  ? Answers on page 265

1 ◆ £100

16

Food is prepared and cooked in which room of the house?

A: Bedroom
B: Kitchen
C: Sitting room
D: Bathroom

17

Which of these is a brand name for a small, portable stereo cassette player?

A: Runman
B: Jogman
C: Walkman
D: Raceman

18

What are the long coarse hairs around the mouth of a cat?

A: Whimpers
B: Whispers
C: Whistles
D: Whiskers

19

Which letter of the alphabet is put at the bottom of an affectionate card?

A: A
B: B
C: X
D: Z

20

What sound is made by a lion?

A: Roar
B: Meow
C: Hoot
D: Howl

50:50 Go to page 241   Go to page 253   ? Answers on page 265

1 ◆ £100

21

Which of these should not be worn on a hot sunny day?

- A: Swimsuit
- B: Shorts
- C: Overcoat
- D: Sunglasses

22

What name is given to the arch of hair above each eye?

- A: Eyelid
- B: Eyelash
- C: Eyebrow
- D: Eyeline

23

Which of these is a game based on tennis, played indoors with small bats and a ball?

- A: Chair tennis
- B: Table tennis
- C: Sofa tennis
- D: Desk tennis

24

What name is given to the plaque on a car showing its registration number?

- A: Number saucer
- B: Number plate
- C: Number dish
- D: Number cup

25

Which of these was invented first?

- A: Computer
- B: Car
- C: Wheel
- D: Radio

 50:50 Go to page 241   Go to page 253    ? Answers on page 265

26

If someone falls over the side of a boat, what is shouted in alarm?

- A: Man underboard
- B: Man sideboard
- C: Man overboard
- D: Man nextboard

27

What mode of transport was used by the early settlers in the days of the American Wild West?

- A: Wagon
- B: Bus
- C: Plane
- D: Spaceship

28

Which of these is shot from a cannon?

- A: Ball
- B: Bat
- C: Bucket
- D: Spade

29

Where are money and valubles left for safekeeping?

- A: Bank
- B: Hospital
- C: Fire station
- D: Police station

30

Which is another name for a photograph?

- A: Snapshot
- B: Potshot
- C: Slingshot
- D: Gunshot

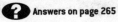 50:50 Go to page 241   Go to page 253   ? Answers on page 265

1 ◆ £100

31

What are birds covered with to keep them warm and help them to fly?

- A: Fur
- B: Hair
- C: Feathers
- D: Wool

32

Which hot brown liquid is often poured over meat before it is eaten?

- A: Bread sauce
- B: Mayonnaise
- C: Gravy
- D: Tomato ketchup

33

How many halves make a whole?

- A: One
- B: Two
- C: Three
- D: Four

34

Which of these is a round, white vegetable with a very strong flavour?

- A: Onion
- B: Carrot
- C: Bean
- D: Beetroot

35

What is the thin part of the leg called where it joins the foot?

- A: Hip
- B: Knee
- C: Ankle
- D: Thigh

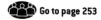 50:50 Go to page 241  Go to page 253 ? Answers on page 265

1 ◆ £100

36

Which month of the year comes
immediately before June?

A: March
B: April
C: July
D: May

37

How many pence are there in a pound?

A: 50
B: 100
C: 150
D: 200

38

Which of these was home to the 'Wonderful Wizard'?

A: Boz
B: Coz
C: Poz
D: Oz

39

In what do birds usually lay their eggs?

A: Cots
B: Cradles
C: Hives
D: Nests

40

Which of these is a stain or a spot?

A: Mark
B: Alan
C: Tony
D: Pete

 50:50 Go to page 241 Go to page 253  **?** Answers on page 265

1 ♦ £100

41

Complete the title of the film: 'The Sound of...'?

A: Singing

B: Whistling

C: Banging

D: Music

42

Which part of your face is used for breathing and smelling?

A: Eyes

B: Ears

C: Mouth

D: Nose

43

How many bears are there in the story of 'Goldilocks'?

A: One

B: Two

C: Three

D: Four

44

Which of these is a garment worn on chilly days?

A: Hopper

B: Jumper

C: Skipper

D: Runner

45

What is caused by a build-up of cars on a road?

A: Traffic spread

B: Traffic marmalade

C: Traffic jam

D: Traffic honey

 50:50 Go to page 241    Go to page 253   ? Answers on page 265

1 ◆ £100

46

Which of these is a red or yellow insect with black spots?

- A: Ladymouse
- B: Ladyfrog
- C: Ladysnail
- D: Ladybird

47

In which of the following is a young kangaroo carried?

- A: Handbag
- B: Pouch
- C: Suitcase
- D: Backpack

48

Which of these is a traditional English breakfast?

- A: Sausage and mash
- B: Fish and chips
- C: Bacon and eggs
- D: Roast beef and Yorkshire pudding

49

Where are clothes taken to be washed?

- A: Launderette
- B: Canteen
- C: Supermarket
- D: Auction

50

Which of these is a tool for cutting wood?

- A: Saw
- B: Heard
- C: Spoke
- D: Listen

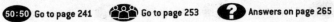 50:50 Go to page 241   Go to page 253   ? Answers on page 265

1 ◆ £100

51

What is the first task after eating a meal?

A: Washing down

B: Washing up

C: Washing in

D: Washing out

52

Which season of the year is associated with the new growth of plants?

A: Spring

B: Summer

C: Autumn

D: Winter

53

Traditionally which animal gives rides on the beach?

A: Cow

B: Camel

C: Elephant

D: Donkey

54

Which of these is a famous children's TV 'Doctor'?

A: Who

B: What

C: Why

D: Where

55

What sort of creature is Babar in the children's books?

A: Giraffe

B: Rhinoceros

C: Lion

D: Elephant

 50:50 Go to page 241   Go to page 253   Answers on page 265

1 ◆ £100

56

Which of these is a hairstyle?

A: Lambtail

B: Horsetail

C: Ponytail

D: Sheeptail

57

Traditionally which of these are put on a birthday cake?

A: Presents

B: Crackers

C: Candles

D: Tinsel

58

Which of these is a shape?

A: Oblong

B: Obshort

C: Obwide

D: Obnarrow

59

Who visited the Seven Dwarfs in their forest home?

A: Sleeping Beauty

B: Thumbelina

C: Goldilocks

D: Snow White

60

Which of these is an area of land where crops are grown and animals are bred?

A: Factory

B: Farm

C: Stables

D: Kennels

50:50 Go to page 241   Go to page 253   ? Answers on page 265

1 ◆ £100

61

What was Humpty Dumpty?

A: Spoon
B: Egg
C: Dish
D: Ball

62

Which garden tool has three or four prongs attached to a handle?

A: Fork
B: Spade
C: Hoe
D: Shears

63

In the nursery rhyme 'Hey Diddle Diddle', who or what jumped over the moon?

A: Cow
B: Cat
C: Dog
D: Rabbit

64

Which of these is a little fish often given as a prize at funfairs?

A: Greenfish
B: Lilacfish
C: Orangefish
D: Goldfish

65

What do children traditionally sit behind at school in order to do their work?

A: Sofa
B: Trolley
C: Chair
D: Desk

 50:50 Go to page 241    Go to page 253   **?** Answers on page 266

1 ◆ £100

66

Which imaginary little being shares
its name with a brand of washing-up liquid?

A: Elf
B: Gnome
C: Fairy
D: Pixie

67

What is a ballerina?

A: Singer
B: Musician
C: Dancer
D: Actor

68

Which dog is often seen working with animals on farms?

A: Horsedog
B: Pigdog
C: Cowdog
D: Sheepdog

69

How many sides has a triangle?

A: 3
B: 4
C: 5
D: 6

70

Which of these is an edible fruit?

A: Red
B: Orange
C: Green
D: Yellow

50:50 Go to page 241   Go to page 253   ? Answers on page 266

1 ◆ £100

71

Who would be most likely to use a wheelbarrow?

A: Painter
B: Mechanic
C: Gardener
D: Chef

72

Which of these means 'clothes that are worn together'?

A: Nearfit
B: Farfit
C: Infit
D: Outfit

73

What is a fried mixture of
flour, eggs and milk called?

A: Panbun
B: Pancake
C: Panbread
D: Panbiscuit

74

Which of these means to steal money
or property from someone else?

A: Steve
B: Tom
C: Rob
D: Alex

75

What name is given to a large garden
area where anyone can walk and play?

A: Place
B: Plant
C: Perch
D: Park

 50:50 Go to page 241    Go to page 253    ? Answers on page 266

1 ◆ £100

Which of these is a piece of furniture in which clothes are kept?

A: Table | B: Wardrobe
C: Bed | D: Chair

What is the last day of the year?

A: 28th December | B: 29th December
C: 30th December | D: 31st December

Which of these is usually played indoors?

A: Table tennis | B: Hockey
C: Rugby | D: Football

What can you see in a zoo?

A: Plants | B: Cars
C: Animals | D: Clothes

Which organ sends messages to the other parts of the body?

A: Brain | B: Heart
C: Lungs | D: Stomach

:50 Go to page 242   Go to page 254   ? Answers on page 266

1 ♦ £100

81

How many noughts are there in the number one thousand?

- A: 2
- B: 3
- C: 4
- D: 5

82

Which attachment on a bicycle is used to attract attention?

- A: Saddle bag
- B: Mudguard
- C: Bell
- D: Basket

83

According to the Bible, who was the mother of Jesus?

- A: Ruth
- B: Elizabeth
- C: Mary
- D: Esther

84

Which of these is a young sheep?

- A: Lamb
- B: Foal
- C: Calf
- D: Kitten

85

Where are ships built and repaired?

- A: Shipinch
- B: Shipfoot
- C: Shipyard
- D: Shipmile

50:50 Go to page 242   Go to page 254   ? Answers on page 266

86

Which of these fruits does not have a stone?

A: Banana

B: Plum

C: Apricot

D: Peach

87

What is put on the front of an envelope
to show where it is going?

A: Map

B: Address

C: Stamp

D: Telephone number

88

Which 'Bunny' first appeared in
American cartoon films in the 1930s?

page
49

A: Grubs

B: Worms

C: Bugs

D: Slugs

50:50		

15	**£1 MILLION**	
14	£500,000	
13	£250,000	
12	£125,000	
11	£64,000	
10	**£32,000**	
9	£16,000	
8	£8,000	
7	£4,000	
6	£2,000	
5	**£1,000**	
4	£500	
3	£300	
2 ◆ £200		
1 ◆ £100		

2 ◆ £200

1

What colour is Marge Simpson's hair?

◆A: Blue

◆B: Green

◆C: Red

◆D: Yellow

2

What name is given to the special clothes worn to school?

◆A: Unishape

◆B: Uniform

◆C: Unifashion

◆D: Unicut

3

What name is given to the storage area in a car?

◆A: Shoe

◆B: Trainer

◆C: Boot

◆D: Plimsoll

4

Where is a car taken to be repaired?

◆A: Garage

◆B: Surgery

◆C: School

◆D: Police station

5

Which piece of jewellery is normally pinned to clothes?

◆A: Bracelet

◆B: Necklace

◆C: Ring

◆D: Brooch

 50:50 Go to page 242   Go to page 254    ? Answers on page 266

2 ◆ £200

6

Christmas Day falls in which month?

A: November   B: December

C: January   D: July

7

On which part of the body would a bonnet be worn?

A: Foot   B: Leg

C: Hand   D: Head

8

What sort of truck is used to lift and move goods?

A: Knife-lift   B: Spoon-lift

C: Fork-lift   D: Slice-lift

9

Which of these is a popular game at parties?

A: Musical chairs   B: Musical tables

C: Musical sofas   D: Musical desks

10

**In folklore, which word means
a person of extraordinary size?**

A: Pixie   B: Fairy

C: Giant   D: Elf

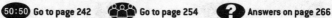 50:50 Go to page 242   Go to page 254   ? Answers on page 266

2 ◆ £200

11

Which is the simplest swimming stroke?

A: Dog paddle | B: Cat paddle
C: Cow paddle | D: Horse paddle

12

How many days are there in a fortnight?

A: 7 | B: 10
C: 14 | D: 20

13

Which of these is a storeroom for food?

A: Loft | B: Pantry
C: Conservatory | D: Hall

14

What name is given to a wobbly, fruit flavoured, clear dessert set with gelatine?

A: Blancmange | B: Yoghurt
C: Jelly | D: Mousse

15

Which of these is not a type of footwear?

A: Shoes | B: Sneakers
C: Shorts | D: Slippers

50:50 Go to page 242   Go to page 254   ? Answers on page 266

2 ◆ £200

16

For what sort of sale are old clothes and toys collected?

- A: Bumble
- B: Jumble
- C: Mumble
- D: Tumble

17

What name is given to the part of the face between the eyebrows and the hairline?

- A: Ear
- B: Forehead
- C: Cheek
- D: Nose

18

Which of these is a hole drilled into the ground to give access to water or oil?

- A: Sound
- B: Fit
- C: Well
- D: Hardy

19

What does the human body do when it becomes too hot?

- A: Sweat
- B: Sneeze
- C: Shiver
- D: Yawn

20

Traditionally, what are pulled at Christmas time?

- A: Snappers
- B: Bangers
- C: Snippers
- D: Crackers

50:50 Go to page 242   Go to page 254   Answers on page 266

2 ◆ £200

21

Which sign shows the way out of a building?

A: Entrance

B: Exit

C: No exit

D: Stop

22

What name is given to the thick, fleshy, rear part of the leg below the knee?

A: Foal

B: Cub

C: Kitten

D: Calf

23

Which of these is a person who makes things out of metal?

A: Jones

B: Smith

C: Brown

D: Grey

24

What is a sleeping compartment on a boat called?

A: Cabin

B: Room

C: Garage

D: Kiosk

25

Which of these is a light, soft cake?

A: Flannel

B: Sponge

C: Brush

D: Loofah

50:50 Go to page 242   Go to page 254   ? Answers on page 266

26

What is the surname of Prince Charles?

A: Smith
B: Evans
C: Windsor
D: Brown

27

Who is the brother of your father or mother?

A: Nephew
B: Cousin
C: Grandfather
D: Uncle

28

Which of these countries shares its name with a Christmas lunch?

A: Greece
B: Romania
C: Turkey
D: Bulgaria

29

Which of these is a popular hand-held computer game?

A: Adventureboy
B: Sportboy
C: Gameboy
D: Hobbyboy

30

What name is given to the title of a front page newspaper article?

A: Armline
B: Legline
C: Headline
D: Footline

50:50 Go to page 242   Go to page 254   Answers on page 266

31

Which of these is a wire or rod that goes from the centre of a wheel to the rim?

- A: Spoke
- B: Said
- C: Wrote
- D: Read

32

Where would you wear a bangle?

- A: Round your neck
- B: Round your head
- C: Round your waist
- D: Round your arm

33

In the Bible, what sort of boat did Noah build?

- A: Tanker
- B: Liner
- C: Ark
- D: Paddleboat

34

What name is given to a person who looks after horses?

- A: Groom
- B: Smarten
- C: Tidy
- D: Comb

35

Which is the tenth letter of the alphabet?

- A: T
- B: M
- C: J
- D: V

50:50 Go to page 242   Go to page 254   **?** Answers on page 266

2 ◆ £200

36

Which word means to chew noisily?

A: Hunch | B: Munch
C: Lunch | D: Bunch

37

Claire and H have left which hugely successful British band to form their own duo?

A: Stairs | B: Ladders
C: Steps | D: Stools

38

Which of these means to walk like a duck?

A: Paddle | B: Muddle
C: Waddle | D: Cuddle

page
59

39

How many sides has a rectangle?

A: 2 | B: 4
C: 6 | D: 8

40

Which attachment on a camera enables photographs to be taken in the dark?

A: Flash | B: Bang
C: Crash | D: Crunch

50:50 Go to page 242   Go to page 254   ? Answers on page 266

41

Where did Toad live in the book 'The Wind in the Willows'?

A: Toad House

B: Toad Palace

C: Toad Hall

D: Toad Castle

42

What name is given to a woman who owns a small hotel and lets rooms?

A: Landmiss

B: Landmother

C: Landlady

D: Landwife

43

Which of these is a snack food consising of a sausage in a bread roll?

A: Hot dog

B: Cold cat

C: Warm weasel

D: Tepid tortoise

44

Golden Delicious and Granny Smith are varieties of which fruit?

A: Apple

B: Orange

C: Banana

D: Plum

45

Which of these animals usually has spots?

A: Leopard

B: Lion

C: Elephant

D: Rhinoceros

50:50 Go to page 242   Go to page 254   Answers on page 266

2 ◆ £200

46

What number is found at the top of a clock face?

- A: 9
- B: 12
- C: 3
- D: 6

47

Which building has a powerful light
which warns and directs ships at sea?

- A: Lightbarn
- B: Lightbungalow
- C: Lightcastle
- D: Lighthouse

48

Where in the house would a duvet normally be found?

- A: On a mantelpiece
- B: On a shelf
- C: On a bed
- D: In the kitchen

49

Which hot drink is a remedy for a cold?

- A: Jam and orange
- B: Honey and lemon
- C: Marmalade and grapefruit
- D: Chocolate spread and grape

50

What name is given to a person
who makes and sells bread and cakes?

- A: Butcher
- B: Grocer
- C: Milkman
- D: Baker

50:50 Go to page 242   Go to page 254   ? Answers on page 266

2 ◆ £200

51

Which of these names is associated with frozen foods?

A: Birdsnose

B: Birdsear

C: Birdseye

D: Birdsneck

52

What is the name of the captain in the 'Tintin' stories?

A: Cod

B: Sardine

C: Tuna

D: Haddock

53

Which of these is a breed of racing dog?

A: Bluehound

B: Blackhound

C: Greyhound

D: Greenhound

54

In the film, what was Chitty-Chitty-Bang-Bang?

A: Drum kit

B: Toy soldier

C: Magical car

D: Cheque book

55

How many days are there in a normal year?

A: 364

B: 365

C: 366

D: 367

50:50 Go to page 242   Go to page 254   ? Answers on page 266

2 ◆ £200

56

Which of these is an even number?

A: 3

B: 5

C: 6

D: 7

57

What is the plural of sheep?

A: Sheep

B: Sheeps

C: Sheepes

D: Sheeppes

58

Which of these words would be first in a dictionary?

page 63

A: Abbey

B: Aberdeen

C: Aardvark

D: Abacus

59

What name is given to the summer allergy that makes some people sneeze and have runny eyes?

A: Straw fever

B: Grass fever

C: Corn fever

D: Hay fever

60

Which of these is an adhesive?

A: String

B: Brown paper

C: Glue

D: Envelope

50:50 Go to page 242   Go to page 254   ? Answers on page 266

61

What colour is a giraffe?

A: Blue and white   **B: Green and white**

C: Brown and white   **D: Red and white**

62

Which of these is a pink-flowered plant?

A: Foxglove   **B: Moleglove**

C: Mouseglove   **D: Ratglove**

63

What time is 20 minutes after 2.45pm?

A: 2.55 pm   **B: 3.25 pm**

C: 3.05 pm   **D: 3.15 pm**

64

Which of these flowers is yellow?

A: Bluebell   **B: Dandelion**

C: Snowdrop   **D: Daisy**

65

What are worn in hockey and cricket to protect the shins?

A: Pods   **B: Pads**

C: Tods   **D: Tads**

 50:50 Go to page 242   Go to page 254    ? Answers on page 266

2 ◆ £200

66

Which of these is not an animal's foot?

A: Paw | B: Trotter
C: Claw | D: Hoof

67

What name is given to a little boy who walks behind the bride at a wedding?

A: Page | B: Paper
C: Cover | D: Book

68

Which of these is not something one can walk on?

A: Path | B: Street
C: Road | D: Canal

69

Complete this line from a well known hymn: 'All things bright and...'?

A: Pretty | B: Beautiful
C: Lovely | D: Attractive

70

What abbreviated title is used before a man's name?

A: Mr | B: Ms
C: Mrs | D: MP

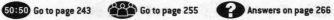 50:50 Go to page 243   Go to page 255   ? Answers on page 266

2 ◆ £200

71

Which of these is a thin, pointed piece of ice which hangs downwards?

A: Icicle

B: Iceberg

C: Icing

D: Ice-cream

72

What letter indicates a hospital on a traffic information sign?

A: E

B: F

C: G

D: H

73

Which is a sleeveless garment often worn over a shirt?

A: Waistcoat

B: Waistjacket

C: Waistjumper

D: Waist-tunic

74

What general name is given to any living being that is not a plant?

A: Bird

B: Reptile

C: Insect

D: Animal

75

Which letter is used to indicate 'yourself'?

A: P

B: I

C: O

D: U

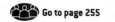 50:50 Go to page 243   Go to page 255   ? Answers on page 266

2 ◆ £200

76

What is a door when it is slightly open?

A: Apot
B: Acan
C: Ajar
D: Ajug

77

Which is the first month of the year to have only thirty days?

A: January
B: February
C: March
D: April

78

What is the piece of cloth or plastic put under a baby's chin to protect its clothes?

page 67

A: Dib
B: Crib
C: Bib
D: Nib

79

Which of these is a book published once a year?

A: Annual
B: Weekly
C: Monthly
D: Daily

80

What is often carried in a pencil case for drawing straight lines and measuring short lengths?

A: Pen
B: Eraser
C: Ruler
D: Pencil sharpener

50:50 Go to page 243   Go to page 255   ? Answers on page 266

2 ◆ £200

81

Which cat chases Jerry the mouse
in the classic TV cartoons?

A: Sylvester
B: Tom
C: Felix
D: Thomasina

82

What type of animal is the fictional
character Paddington?

A: Dog
B: Cat
C: Pony
D: Bear

83

Which musical instrument does
the cartoon character Lisa Simpson play?

A: Trumpet
B: Saxophone
C: Piano
D: Drums

84

When you feel a little depressed and
sad you are said to be 'down in the...'?

A: Dumps
B: Mumps
C: Lumps
D: Pumps

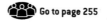 50:50 Go to page 243   Go to page 255    ? Answers on page 266

15 **£1 MILLION**

14 £500,000

13 £250,000

12 £125,000

11 £64,000

10 **£32,000**

9 £16,000

8 £8,000

7 £4,000

6 £2,000

5 **£1,000**

4 £500

3 ◆ £300

2 ◆ £200

1 ◆ £100

3 ◆ £300

1

Which of these is a food strainer used in the kitchen?

A: Calendar
B: Colander
C: Collier
D: Cellophane

2

What name is given to the bars at the front and back of a car to protect it?

A: Bumpers
B: Mumpers
C: Lumpers
D: Dumpers

3

Which of these is a satellite TV system?

A: Ocean
B: Earth
C: Sun
D: Sky

4

What name is given to the special chair used by kings and queens?

A: Stool
B: Throne
C: Sofa
D: Bench

5

Which of Winnie-the-Pooh's friends likes to bounce?

A: Eeyore
B: Piglet
C: Rabbit
D: Tigger

50:50 Go to page 243    Go to page 255    Answers on page 266

6

What is the day immediately before today?

- A: Tomorrow
- B: Yesterday
- C: Last week
- D: Tomorrow fortnight

7

Which of these is a male goat?

- A: Andy goat
- B: Billy goat
- C: Sammy goat
- D: Harry goat

8

What name is given to someone who trains others in sport?

- A: Bus
- B: Coach
- C: Caravan
- D: Cab

9

Which of these is a dome-shaped house made with blocks of snow and ice?

- A: Tent
- B: Bungalow
- C: Igloo
- D: Flat

10

What is stored in a library?

- A: Hats
- B: Hay
- C: Balls
- D: Books

50:50 Go to page 243   Go to page 255   ? Answers on page 266

3 ◆ £300

11

Which of these cannot be made from milk?

A: Cheese

B: Eggs

C: Butter

D: Cream

12

How many days are there in the month of September?

A: 28

B: 29

C: 30

D: 31

13

What is traditionally carried by a fairy?

A: Baton

B: Wand

C: Cane

D: Stick

14

Which of these is a garment similar to a sweater?

A: Pullunder

B: Pullover

C: Pullup

D: Pullon

15

John, Paul, George and Ringo were all members of which pop group?

A: The Beatles

B: The Butterflies

C: The Ladybirds

D: The Dragonflies

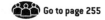 50:50 Go to page 243   Go to page 255    ? Answers on page 266

3 ♦ £300

16

Which of these are well-known sweets?

A: Clever clogs
B: Smarties
C: Know it alls
D: Boffins

17

When swimming, what is worn to protect the eyes?

A: Spectacles
B: Goggles
C: Monocle
D: Binoculars

18

Which of these is a book without a hard cover?

A: Paperback
B: Silkfront
C: Woolside
D: Ironbottom

19

What transports people up and down between the floors of a building?

A: Raise
B: Lift
C: Hoist
D: Winch

20

Which of these is the long hair growing from a horse's neck?

A: Whisker
B: Mane
C: Beard
D: Down

50:50 Go to page 243   Go to page 255   ? Answers on page 266

3 ◆ £300

21

What is the creature in Roald Dahl's book 'The BFG'?

A: Ogre
B: Fairy
C: Imp
D: Giant

22

Which of these is a large ship for carrying oil?

A: Rig
B: Slick
C: Tanker
D: Well

23

A fawn is the young of which animal?

A: Cat
B: Dog
C: Horse
D: Deer

24

Which musical instrument shares its name with an ice cream cone?

A: Flute
B: Oboe
C: Cornet
D: Bassoon

25

In the Bible, what were written by Matthew, Mark, Luke and John?

A: Letters
B: Psalms
C: Gospels
D: Proverbs

50:50 Go to page 243 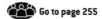 Go to page 255  Answers on page 266

3 ◆ £300

26

Which of these precious stones is a shade of green?

- A: Ruby
- B: Diamond
- C: Sapphire
- D: Emerald

27

What shape is a boxing ring?

- A: Circle
- B: Square
- C: Oval
- D: Triangle

28

Which of these is a classic 'whodunit' board game?

- A: Master key
- B: Decipher
- C: Cluedo
- D: Fathom

29

According to the Highway Code, what should
children be taught to help them cross the road?

- A: Red Circle code
- B: Green Cross code
- C: Blue Square code
- D: Yellow Triangle code

30

Which word means a single step?

- A: Speed
- B: Pace
- C: Rate
- D: Race

50:50 Go to page 243   Go to page 255   ? Answers on page 266

3 ◆ £300

31
What is another name for a taxi?

A: Dab
B: Cab
C: Fab
D: Tab

32
Which word is used for a division of the school year?

A: Chapter
B: Term
C: Section
D: Month

33
Where would a cactus grow?

A: On an iceberg
B: In a rain forest
C: In a hot desert
D: On the sea shore

34
Which of these is a racket sport?

A: Smash
B: Squash
C: Wreck
D: Crush

35
What are magic words spoken to make things happen?

A: Reads
B: Writes
C: Spells
D: Adds

50:50 Go to page 243   Go to page 255   ? Answers on page 266

3 ◆ £300

36

Which tree shares its name with the powder which is left after something has been burnt?

A: Oak
B: Elm
C: Ash
D: Holly

37

What are the first two words of the Lord's Prayer?

A: Dear Lord
B: Our Father
C: Jesus Christ
D: Holy God

38

Which sport shares its name with a word meaning 'browsing the Internet'?

A: Swimming
B: Diving
C: Skiing
D: Surfing

39

What sort of grocer sells fruit and vegetables?

A: Orange
B: Lilac
C: Green
D: Maroon

40

Which of these is the area at a football ground on which the game takes place?

A: Green
B: Wicket
C: Pitch
D: Court

50:50 Go to page 243   Go to page 255   ? Answers on page 266

41

What is the glove puppet Sooty?

A: Panda

B: Dog

C: Polar bear

D: Teddy bear

42

Which of these is a popular lemon and lime flavoured soft drink?

A: 6 UP

B: 7 UP

C: 8 UP

D: 9 UP

43

How many people are involved in a solo performance?

A: Four

B: Three

C: Two

D: One

44

Which of these is a flat, rectangular case for carrying books and papers?

A: Shortbag

B: Briefbox

C: Shortcrate

D: Briefcase

45

According to the saying, what 'keeps the doctor away'?

A: An orange a day

B: An apple a day

C: A pear a day

D: A banana a day

50:50 Go to page 243 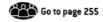 Go to page 255  Answers on page 266

46

Which of these is a suspended seat
used for carrying skiers uphill?

- A: Chairlift
- B: Benchlift
- C: Sofalift
- D: Seatlift

47

The national flag of the United Kingdom
is known as the Union...?

- A: Jack
- B: Jill
- C: Bill
- D: Ben

48

Which of these is a brightly coloured
bird that lives near rivers?

- A: Queenfarmer
- B: Princeshooter
- C: Kingfisher
- D: Princessgardener

49

In Scotland, what is a loch?

- A: Hill
- B: River
- C: Lake
- D: Town

50

Which is the highest valued
medal at the Olympic Games?

- A: Bronze
- B: Silver
- C: Brass
- D: Gold

50:50 Go to page 243   Go to page 255   ? Answers on page 266

3 ◆ £300

51

What name is given to someone who talks all the time?

A: Chatterbag | B: Chatterball
C: Chatterbeg | D: Chatterbox

52

Which 'Street' is a famous TV soap?

A: Abdication | B: Carnation
C: Coronation | D: Decoration

53

What 'colour' are you said to be when you are feeling sad?

A: Blue | B: Red
C: Yellow | D: Green

54

Who helps Santa Claus prepare the presents?

A: Elves | B: Fairies
C: Goblins | D: Pixies

55

Which film was a British box office hit in 2001?

A: Cats and Dogs | B: Rats and Mice
C: Rabbits and Hares | D: Horses and Donkeys

3 ◆ £300

56

What is the name of Walt Disney's famous little elephant?

- A: Bimbo
- B: Dumbo
- C: Jumbo
- D: Mumbo

57

Which little flowers are traditionally used to make 'chains'?

- A: Snowdrops
- B: Dandelions
- C: Roses
- D: Daisies

58

What would help a sick or injured person before a doctor arrived?

- A: First-aid
- B: Second-aid
- C: Third-aid
- D: Fourth-aid

59

Which sort of bird can often be taught to speak?

- A: Eagle
- B: Ostrich
- C: Parrot
- D: Robin

60

What is the name of the TV detective played by David Jason?

- A: Sleet
- B: Frost
- C: Ice
- D: Snow

 **50:50** Go to page 243   **** Go to page 255   **?** Answers on page 266

3 ◆ £300

61

Which of these is not a country?

A: USA
B: Australia
C: Africa
D: France

62

What name is given to the part of a stove where food is roasted or baked?

A: Grill
B: Oven
C: Warming drawer
D: Hot plate

63

Which of these is a common flying insect?

A: Mummy longlegs
B: Daddy longlegs
C: Grandma longlegs
D: Grandpa longlegs

64

A caterpillar is the larva of which insect?

A: Wasp
B: Bee
C: Beetle
D: Butterfly

65

Which 'tug' is a contest between two teams pulling a rope from opposite ends?

A: Tug-of-war
B: Tug-of-battle
C: Tug-of-fight
D: Tug-of-combat

50:50 Go to page 244 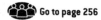 Go to page 256  Answers on page 266

3 ♦ £300

66

What colour is the fur of a polar bear?

- A: Black
- B: Brown
- C: White
- D: Red

67

Which famous historical character gave his name to a long waterproof rubber boot?

- A: Nelson
- B: Wellington
- C: Churchill
- D: Napoleon

68

What do your feet push on to make a bicycle move?

- A: Pedals
- B: Handlebars
- C: Wheel
- D: Pump

69

In the UK, what title is given to the daughter of a king or queen?

- A: Princess
- B: Lady
- C: Duchess
- D: Dame

70

Which word means slightly warm?

- A: Dalewarm
- B: Deanwarm
- C: Lloydwarm
- D: Lukewarm

50:50 Go to page 244　　Go to page 256　　Answers on page 266

71

What name is given to the legal document which sets out what is to happen to someone's money and property after their death?

A: Sam   B: Will

C: Pete   D: Don

72

Which of these is a holiday for a newly married couple after their wedding?

A: Honeysun   B: Honeystar

C: Honeymoon   D: Honeyplanet

73

How many hours are there in one day?

A: 4   B: 14

C: 24   D: 48

74

Which character did Harrison Ford play in a series of famous films?

A: Indiana Smith   B: Indiana Jones

C: Indiana Brown   D: Indiana Evans

75

What name is given to a nil score in tennis?

A: Love   B: Nought

C: Blank   D: Nothing

 50:50 Go to page 244   Go to page 256   ? Answers on page 266

3 ◆ £300

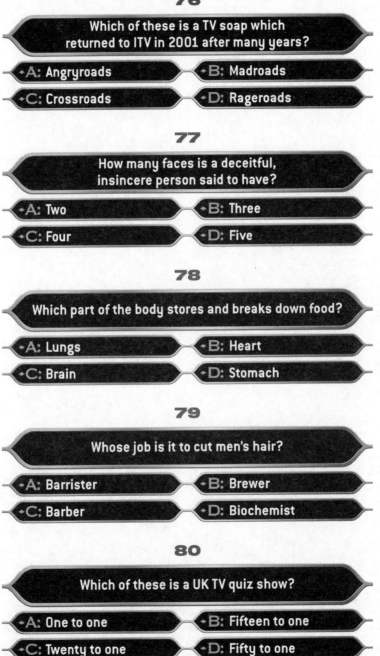

76

Which of these is a TV soap which returned to ITV in 2001 after many years?

- A: Angryroads
- B: Madroads
- C: Crossroads
- D: Rageroads

77

How many faces is a deceitful, insincere person said to have?

- A: Two
- B: Three
- C: Four
- D: Five

78

Which part of the body stores and breaks down food?

page 85

- A: Lungs
- B: Heart
- C: Brain
- D: Stomach

79

Whose job is it to cut men's hair?

- A: Barrister
- B: Brewer
- C: Barber
- D: Biochemist

80

Which of these is a UK TV quiz show?

- A: One to one
- B: Fifteen to one
- C: Twenty to one
- D: Fifty to one

50:50 Go to page 244   Go to page 256   ? Answers on page 266

50:50

15	£1 MILLION
14	£500,000
13	£250,000
12	£125,000
11	£64,000
10	£32,000
9	£16,000
8	£8,000
7	£4,000
6	£2,000
5	£1,000
4 ◆	£500
3 ◆	£300
2 ◆	£200
1 ◆	£100

4 ◆ £500

1

What is the American word for a biscuit?

A: Rookie

B: Cookie

C: Bookie

D: Quickie

2

Which outlaw who 'stole from the rich to give to the poor' had a band of Merry Men?

A: Robin Hat

B: Robin Cap

C: Robin Hood

D: Robin Bonnet

3

Which of these is a popular TV cartoon series?

A: Bob the Builder

B: Pete the Plumber

C: Gordon the Gardener

D: Paul the Painter

4

Which of the following is a chain of fast food restaurants?

A: McNaughton's

B: McBride's

C: McTavish's

D: McDonald's

5

What are crossed to keep away bad omens and bring good luck?

A: Fingers

B: Toes

C: Legs

D: Arms

4 ◆ £500

6

Which of these is a place where coal is dug out of the ground?

A: Yours   B: His

C: Ours   D: Mine

7

According to the Bible, who was the first man on Earth?

A: Adam   B: Solomon

C: Isaac   D: Moses

8

Which kitchen utensil is used to roll out dough?

A: Rolling nail   B: Rolling tack

C: Rolling stone   D: Rolling pin

9

In the story 'The Three Little Pigs', with what did the first little pig build his house?

A: Feathers   B: Sticks

C: Straw   D: Bricks

10

Which of these musical instruments is blown?

A: Violin   B: Piano

C: Guitar   D: Flute

50:50 Go to page 244   Go to page 256   ? Answers on page 267

4 ◆ £500

11
What nickname is given to the world's largest passenger plane?

A: Giant jet
B: Jumbo jet
C: Mega jet
D: Super jet

12
Which of these is a large letter at the beginning of a sentence?

A: Capital
B: Basic
C: Italic
D: Mark

13
In painting, which colour is a mixture of blue and yellow?

A: Purple
B: Green
C: Red
D: Brown

14
What word means the straw and hay used as bedding for animals?

A: Rubbish
B: Litter
C: Trash
D: Junk

15
Traditionally what container is used for storing biscuits?

A: Barrel
B: Box
C: Jar
D: Can

50:50 Go to page 244   Go to page 256   ? Answers on page 267

4 ◆ £500

16

What is the official currency of the USA?

◆A: Franc ◆B: Lira

◆C: Dollar ◆D: Pound

17

Which of these is 'meat on a stick'?

◆A: Kebub ◆B: Kebeb

◆C: Kebib ◆D: Kebab

18

Who is directly in charge of the animals in a zoo?

◆A: Janitor ◆B: Keeper

◆C: Trainer ◆D: Jailer

19

Which of these is a short-lived fashion?

◆A: Had ◆B: Fad

◆C: Lad ◆D: Bad

20

Where on the body would a shawl usually be worn?

◆A: Shoulders ◆B: Feet

◆C: Legs ◆D: Hands

50:50 Go to page 244   Go to page 256   ? Answers on page 267

4 ◆ £500

21

Which planet shares its name with a chocolate bar?

A: Uranus
B: Venus
C: Pluto
D: Mars

22

Who is the only member of a football team who is allowed to handle the ball whilst it is in play?

A: Sweeper
B: Wing
C: Goalkeeper
D: Centre forward

23

How many lives is a cat said to have?

A: 5
B: 7
C: 9
D: 10

24

Which of these is a soft, toffee-like sweet made from butter, cream and sugar?

A: Fudge
B: Marzipan
C: Nougat
D: Sherbet

25

What are often worn instead of stockings?

A: Shorts
B: Tights
C: Baggies
D: Longs

50:50 Go to page 244   Go to page 256   Answers on page 267

4 ◆ £500

26

Which word describes the moon when it is a complete circle?

A: New
B: Half
C: Crescent
D: Full

27

What are you doing to two numbers if you put a '+' sign between them?

A: Subtracting
B: Adding
C: Multiplying
D: Dividing

28

Which word means to change TV channels frequently using a remote control?

A: Wap
B: Zip
C: Zap
D: Pang

29

What name is given to the hole in the top of a needle through which the cotton is threaded?

A: Mouth
B: Eye
C: Nose
D: Ear

30

Which is the only month of the year not to consist of 30 or 31 days?

A: September
B: May
C: February
D: July

50:50 Go to page 244   Go to page 256   ? Answers on page 267

4 ◆ £500

31

What name is given to unidentified flying objects?

A: Flying plates

B: Flying saucers

C: Flying dishes

D: Flying frisbees

32

Which of these is a knitted garment
worn on the upper part of the body?

A: Isle of Man

B: Isle of Skye

C: Jersey

D: Anglesey

33

What is a thick, smooth sauce made
with tomatoes, spices and vinegar?

A: Mayonnaise

B: Pickle

C: Chutney

D: Ketchup

34

Which of these is a type of music
first heard in the 1950s?

A: Pebble

B: Stone

C: Rock

D: Boulder

35

In football, what name is given to a quick
move of the ball from one player to another?

A: Fail

B: Pass

C: Run

D: Overtake

50:50 Go to page 244 Go to page 256  ? Answers on page 267

4 ◆ £500

36

What is the name of Walt Disney's 2001 film about a destroyed city?

A: Mulan

B: Toy Story

C: Little Mermaid

D: Atlantis: The Lost Empire

37

Which of these is a breed of dog?

A: French farmer

B: German shepherd

C: Swiss salesman

D: Greek grocer

38

What was the nickname of King Richard I of England?

A: Lionheart

B: Giraffeneck

C: Mousebrain

D: Pigear

39

Which of these is a long running television music programme?

A: Pop of the Tops

B: Top of the Tips

C: Top of the Pops

D: Tip of the Tops

40

What colour is Thomas the Tank Engine?

A: Blue

B: Green

C: Red

D: Yellow

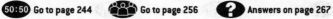
50:50 Go to page 244   Go to page 256   ? Answers on page 267

4 ◆ £500

41

Which of these is a popular children's party game?

- A: Salmon
- B: Sardines
- C: Trout
- D: Herring

42

What name is given to Italian flat baked dough served with various toppings?

- A: Pitta
- B: Pavlova
- C: Paella
- D: Pizza

43

When are painted or chocolate eggs traditionally given?

- A: Christmas
- B: Birthday
- C: Easter
- D: Bonfire night

44

Which word has come to mean models who have become celebrities in their own right?

- A: Supermodel
- B: Fantasticmodel
- C: Wizzomodel
- D: Brilliantmodel

45

What is a junior Scout called?

- A: Kid
- B: Calf
- C: Cub
- D: Kitten

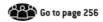 50:50 Go to page 244   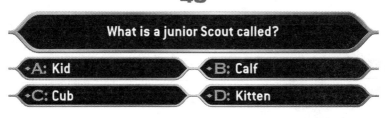 Go to page 256    Answers on page 267

4 ◆ £500

46

Which of these is a famous car, first manufactured in 1959 and re-launched in 2001?

A: Tiny
B: Teeny
C: Weeny
D: Mini

47

Who is Barbie's boyfriend?

A: Will
B: Bill
C: Ben
D: Ken

48

Which of these is a pirate's currency?

A: Pieces of two
B: Pieces of four
C: Pieces of six
D: Pieces of eight

49

What colour is beetroot?

A: Green
B: Yellow
C: Blue
D: Red

50

Which of these is a female pig?

A: Plant
B: Dig
C: Sow
D: Weed

4 ◆ £500

51

What name is given to the cooking of food on metal bars, put under or over the heat?

- A: Boiling
- B: Grilling
- C: Steaming
- D: Frying

52

Which of these is an old Spanish sailing ship?

- A: Gallon
- B: Gallery
- C: Gallop
- D: Galleon

53

How many centimetres are there in 1 metre?

- A: 25
- B: 50
- C: 75
- D: 100

54

What, in our solar system, gives us light and keeps us warm?

- A: Sun
- B: Moon
- C: Stars
- D: Sky

55

Which of these was not related to Peter Rabbit?

- A: Flopsy
- B: Mopsy
- C: Cottontail
- D: Simon

 50:50 Go to page 244   Go to page 256    ? Answers on page 267

4 ◆ £500

56

What sort of pies are traditionally eaten at Christmas time?

A: Mince
B: Chop
C: Split
D: Tear

57

How many quarters are there in a half?

A: One
B: Two
C: Three
D: Four

page 99

58

What colour are lavender flowers?

A: Pale yellow
B: Pale purple
C: Pale green
D: Brown

59

Which word is used when asking a question relating to a place?

A: Who
B: What
C: Where
D: When

60

What sort of 'rats' can be seen in a TV cartoon series?

A: Carpetrats
B: Tilerats
C: Matrats
D: Rugrats

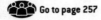 50:50 Go to page 244   Go to page 257   ? Answers on page 267

61

Which room or building has tools and machinery used for making and repairing things?

◆A: Market | ◆B: Corner shop
◆C: Office | ◆D: Workshop

62

What name is given to the building where plays are performed on a stage?

◆A: Arena | ◆B: Theatre
◆C: Stadium | ◆D: Gallery

63

How many years are there in half a century?

◆A: 25 | ◆B: 50
◆C: 75 | ◆D: 100

64

Which of these is another way of writing '25 minutes to 9'?

◆A: 9.15 | ◆B: 8.35
◆C: 8.45 | ◆D: 9.35

65

What name is given to this punctuation mark: - ?

◆A: Dash | ◆B: Rush
◆C: Run | ◆D: Hurry

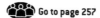 **50:50** Go to page 245   Go to page 257   **?** Answers on page 267

4 ◆ £500

66

Which of these is a method of making clothes from wool?

A: Knit

B: Knat

C: Knack

D: Knock

67

According to the nursery rhyme, who was 'quite contrary'?

A: 'Sally, Sally'

B: 'Mary, Mary'

C: 'Sophie, Sophie'

D: 'Louise, Louise'

68

Which two letters are shown to be missing by the apostrophe in the word 'can't'?

A: NA

B: NE

C: NI

D: NO

69

Who is the father of Prince William and Prince Harry?

A: Prince Cuthbert

B: Prince Charles

C: Prince Conrad

D: Prince Craig

70

Which of these is not a UK television channel?

A: BBC 1

B: BBC 2

C: BBC 5

D: Channel 5

50:50 Go to page 245 Go to page 257 ? Answers on page 267

4 ◆ £500

71

What is the main colour of a road 'STOP' sign?

- A: Red
- B: Blue
- C: Green
- D: Yellow

72

In which profession has Sir Elton John become famous?

- A: Singing
- B: Dancing
- C: Acting
- D: Magic

73

Where on the body is a bracelet worn?

- A: Waist
- B: Neck
- C: Head
- D: Wrist

74

Which of these is a proper noun?

- A: Country
- B: Ocean
- C: Spain
- D: Sea

75

Which sort of windows lead from a house into a garden?

- A: English
- B: German
- C: Spanish
- D: French

50:50 Go to page 245   Go to page 257   ? Answers on page 267

4 ◆ £500

What was the surname of the American rock and roll singing legend, Elvis?

◆A: Porter

◆B: Priestley

◆C: Potter

◆D: Presley

50:50 Go to page 245   Go to page 257   ? Answers on page 267

50:50

15	**£1 MILLION**
14	£500,000
13	£250,000
12	£125,000
11	£64,000
10	**£32,000**
9	£16,000
8	£8,000
7	£4,000
6	£2,000
5 ◆	**£1,000**
4 ◆	£500
3 ◆	£300
2 ◆	£200
1 ◆	£100

5 ◆ £1,000

1

Which pudding traditionally accompanies roast beef?

A: Lancashire

B: Dorset

C: Devon

D: Yorkshire

2

In golf, what name is given to the sticks used to hit the balls?

A: Hearts

B: Clubs

C: Diamonds

D: Spades

3

Which of these is a popular toy with a spool and string?

A: So-so

B: Do-do

C: Yo-yo

D: No-no

4

What is the name of the candy stick sold at the seaside?

A: Rock

B: Chunk

C: Slab

D: Stone

5

Which word means 'in another country'?

A: Awide

B: Abroad

C: Athick

D: Afat

50:50 Go to page 245   Go to page 257   **?** Answers on page 267

5 ◆ £1,000

6

How many minutes are there in two and a half hours?

A: 60

B: 90

C: 120

D: 150

7

Which of these is a green fruit that can be cooked and eaten?

A: Mouseberry

B: Turkeyberry

C: Gooseberry

D: Catberry

8

Who is Batman's 'Boy Wonder'?

A: Richard

B: Robin

C: Ronald

D: Ray

9

Which 'roll' is a thin cake of sponge filled with jam and cream?

A: French

B: German

C: Swiss

D: Welsh

10

What name is given to the person who operates the controls of an aeroplane?

A: Driver

B: Navigator

C: Pilot

D: Conductor

50:50 Go to page 245   Go to page 257   ? Answers on page 267

5 ◆ £1,000

11

Which of these is an illness with red, itchy spots?

- A: Turkeypox
- B: Chickenpox
- C: Swanpox
- D: Goosepox

12

What sort of truck would you see on a building site?

- A: Thumper
- B: Dumper
- C: Loafer
- D: Woofer

13

Which of these numbers is not a multiple of 7?

- A: 28
- B: 49
- C: 77
- D: 54

14

What is another name for the teeth which snakes use to inject venom into their prey?

- A: Sting
- B: Fang
- C: Claw
- D: Node

15

Which of these is a type of pastry?

- A: Blow
- B: Puff
- C: Gasp
- D: Pant

50:50 Go to page 245   Go to page 257   ? Answers on page 267

5 ◆ £1,000

16

What sort of nurse is trained to help women during pregnancy and the birth of their baby?

◆A: Farwife   ◆B: Midwife

◆C: Closewife   ◆D: Nextwife

17

Which of these is a disease often caught by children?

◆A: German measles   ◆B: French measles

◆C: English measles   ◆D: Dutch measles

18

Who is Prince William's younger brother?

◆A: Prince Hubert   ◆B: Prince Howard

◆C: Prince Harold   ◆D: Prince Harry

19

Which of these is a general name for some parts of the human body?

◆A: Piano   ◆B: Organ

◆C: Banjo   ◆D: Guitar

20

What sort of bird is Big Bird from Sesame Street?

◆A: Parrot   ◆B: Toucan

◆C: Budgerigar   ◆D: Canary

 50:50 Go to page 245   Go to page 257   ? Answers on page 267

5 ◆ £1,000

21

Which of these is not a fish?

- A: Salmon
- B: Spat
- C: Trout
- D: Tuna

22

What sort of tale is thought to be foolish and unscientific?

- A: Ancient husband's
- B: Old wives'
- C: Elder brother's
- D: Senior sister's

23

Which of these is a famous high street chemist?

- A: Boots
- B: Shoes
- C: Slippers
- D: Wellies

24

What are sometimes worn instead of spectacles?

- A: Contact lenses
- B: Goggles
- C: Face mask
- D: Visor

25

In the olden days what name was given to the thick skewer on which meat cooked over a fire?

- A: Cough
- B: Splutter
- C: Spit
- D: Choke

50:50 Go to page 245   Go to page 257   ? Answers on page 267

5 ◆ £1,000

26

Which of these is a successful pop group?

◆A: S Club 7 | B: T Club 8
◆C: V Club 9 | D: R Club 6

27

What name is given to the most important town or city in a country?

◆A: Chief | B: Main
◆C: Prime | D: Capital

28

Which is another word for Christmas?

page 111

◆A: Mule | B: Yule
◆C: Rule | D: Zule

29

Most water birds have what sort of feet?

◆A: Hooked | B: Webbed
◆C: Plaited | D: Laced

30

What forms in the body to stop bleeding?

◆A: Twit | B: Clot
◆C: Fool | D: Mug

 50:50 Go to page 245   Go to page 257    ? Answers on page 267

5 ◆ £1,000

31

Which part of an envelope has to be stuck
down before it is put in the postbox?

A: Flop

B: Flip

C: Flap

D: Fly

32

What name is given to a ball which
is covered with a map of the world?

A: Sphere

B: Round

C: Earth

D: Globe

33

Which chocolate bar shares its name
with a huge mass of stars?

A: Crunchie

B: Galaxy

C: Twix

D: Snickers

34

What sort of face are you said to have
when you are disappointed and miserable?

A: Short

B: Wide

C: Thin

D: Long

35

Which of these is a popular attraction at village fetes?

A: Fortunate fumble

B: Happy handful

C: Lucky dip

D: Good chance

50:50 Go to page 245   Go to page 257   Answers on page 267

5 ◆ £1,000

36

What is the title of the Christmas 2001
No 1 hit by Robbie Williams and Nicole Kidman?

A: Some are silly

B: Everything's easy

C: No nonsense

D: Something stupid

37

Which of these is a famous Hollywood actor?

A: Clint Westwood

B: Clint Northwood

C: Clint Eastwood

D: Clint Southwood

38

What is the name of the large island
to the northwest of Iceland?

A: Blueland

B: Redland

C: Greenland

D: Blackland

39

Which of these is not a vegetable?

A: Carrot

B: Cabbage

C: Cashew

D: Cauliflower

40

What can be added to food to give it a distinctive taste?

A: Colouring

B: Water

C: Flavouring

D: Thickener

50:50 Go to page 245   Go to page 257   ? Answers on page 267

5 ◆ £1,000

41

Which of these is a compound noun?

A: Shop
B: Department store
C: Hotel
D: Inn

42

What is the highest number that can be thrown with three normal dice?

A: 30
B: 12
C: 18
D: 24

43

Which of these prefixes means 'wrong'?

A: Mid
B: Mini
C: Mis
D: Mono

44

What name is given to a safety device in an electrical circuit?

A: Fuse
B: Wire
C: Plug
D: Socket

45

In which musical do the characters Fagin, Bill Sikes and the Artful Dodger appear?

A: Benjamin!
B: Oliver!
C: Simon!
D: Ashley!

50:50 Go to page 245  Go to page 257  Answers on page 267

5 ◆ £1,000

46

Who hosts a programme of music on the radio
or TV, or plays music in dance clubs?

A: AJ

B: BJ

C: CJ

D: DJ

47

Which of these sea creatures lives in a double shell?

A: Shark

B: Octopus

C: Oyster

D: Crab

48

What name is given to a group of wolves?

A: Store

B: Pack

C: Crowd

D: Club

49

Which of these is not an ocean?

A: Indian

B: African

C: Atlantic

D: Pacific

50

Complete the title of the book: 'The Wind in the...'?

A: Oaks

B: Elms

C: Willows

D: Beeches

50:50 Go to page 245   Go to page 257   ? Answers on page 267

5 ◆ £1,000

51

Which of these is not a type of bread?

A: Wholemeal

B: White

C: Granite

D: Pitta

52

What type of musical instrument is the flute?

A: Brass

B: Woodwind

C: String

D: Percussion

53

Which of these is not part of a car?

A: Wing

B: Bonnet

C: Boot

D: Head

54

How is the fraction ½ written as a decimal?

A: 0.25

B: 0.5

C: 0.75

D: 0.99

55

Which of these is not a seat?

A: Settee

B: Settle

C: Sofa

D: Shack

50:50 Go to page 245   Go to page 257   ? Answers on page 267

5 ◆ £1,000

56

If something trebles, how many times greater does it become?

- ◆ A: 2
- ◆ B: 3
- ◆ C: 4
- ◆ D: 5

57

Which of these is a small glass container used in chemical experiments?

- ◆ A: Test wire
- ◆ B: Test pipe
- ◆ C: Test cylinder
- ◆ D: Test tube

58

What name is given to a book or film that tells an exciting story about dangerous or mysterious events?

- ◆ A: Creeper
- ◆ B: Tickler
- ◆ C: Thriller
- ◆ D: Tingler

59

Which of these are films about North America in the 19th and early 20th centuries?

- ◆ A: Northerns
- ◆ B: Southerns
- ◆ C: Westerns
- ◆ D: Easterns

60

In the lullaby 'Hush-a-bye, baby', where was the cradle placed?

- ◆ A: On the tree top
- ◆ B: By the water's edge
- ◆ C: In a flower garden
- ◆ D: Below the waterfall

50:50 Go to page 245   Go to page 258   ? Answers on page 267

5 ◆ £1,000

61

Which of these is a piece of clothing worn to protect other clothes whilst working?

A: Oversome
B: Overany
C: Overfew
D: Overall

62

Where would a thimble be worn?

A: On the head
B: Around the neck
C: On a finger
D: On a toe

63

What is a large indoor area for ice skating or roller skating called?

A: Ring
B: Rink
C: Arena
D: Playground

64

In grammar, which is the 'first person'?

A: I
B: You
C: He
D: She

65

Which of these French words can mean 'sorry'?

A: Revue
B: Parley
C: Pardon
D: Grace

50:50 Go to page 246   Go to page 258   **?** Answers on page 267

5 ◆ £1,000

66

What sort of friend lives far away but is written to regularly?

A: Crayon
B: Pen
C: Pencil
D: Chalk

67

Jim Davidson is associated with which TV game show?

A: The Price is Right
B: The Generation Game
C: Family Fortunes
D: Supermarket Sweep

68

What name is given to the place where traffic is allowed to drive across a railway track?

A: Straight crossing
B: Direct crossing
C: Level crossing
D: Flat crossing

69

Which European country is particularly associated with pasta?

A: France
B: England
C: Spain
D: Italy

70

What is the normal UK speed limit in a built-up area?

A: 30 mph
B: 40 mph
C: 50 mph
D: 60 mph

50:50 Go to page 246   Go to page 258   ? Answers on page 267

5 ◆ £1,000

71

Home to Hollywood, the city of
Los Angeles is in which country?

◆A: England ◆B: France

◆C: Australia ◆D: USA

72

What name is given to the person
who directs an orchestra?

◆A: Driver ◆B: Conductor

◆C: Navigator ◆D: Pilot

50:50 Go to page 246 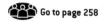 Go to page 258  Answers on page 267

50:50

15 **£1 MILLION**

14 £500,000

13 £250,000

12 £125,000

11 £64,000

10 **£32,000**

9 £16,000

8 £8,000

7 £4,000

6 ◆ **£2,000**

5 ◆ £1,000

4 ◆ £500

3 ◆ £300

2 ◆ £200

1 ◆ £100

6 ◆ £2,000

1

What is the French word for 'yes'?

A: Da
B: Oui
C: Ja
D: Si

2

Which of these is a place where monks or nuns live and work?

A: Abbey
B: Castle
C: Palace
D: Church

3

Food that is prepared and served quickly is known as what?

A: Rapid
B: Fast
C: Swift
D: Snappy

4

Which creature lives in water and resembles a small tortoise?

A: Terrapin
B: Terrapod
C: Terrapill
D: Terrapad

5

In the story of Aladdin, in what does the genie live?

A: Box
B: Lamp
C: Wardrobe
D: Bag

50:50 Go to page 246   Go to page 258   Answers on page 267

6 ◆ £2,000

6

Who would clean teeth at the dentist's surgery?

A: Hygienist

B: Receptionist

C: Secretary

D: Telephonist

7

What sort of a kart is a very simple racing vehicle, often used on special circuits?

A: Go

B: Stop

C: Left

D: Right

8

Who was the first Englishman to sail round the world?

A: Francis Duck

B: Francis Swan

C: Francis Drake

D: Francis Gull

9

Which of the following is not part of the United Kingdom?

A: Eire

B: Scotland

C: Wales

D: England

10

What name is given to the early times when people lived in caves and began to make tools?

A: Stone Age

B: Pebble Age

C: Boulder Age

D: Rock Age

50:50 Go to page 246   Go to page 258   ? Answers on page 267

6 ◆ £2,000

11

Scotland is famous for which alcoholic drink?

- A: Rum
- B: Whisky
- C: Gin
- D: Vodka

12

What name is given to a number
one playing card in a pack?

- A: Jack
- B: Queen
- C: King
- D: Ace

13

Which of these is the hollow
underneath the top of the arm?

- A: Armpit
- B: Armhole
- C: Armslot
- D: Armtube

14

What name is given to a room
built inside the roof of a house?

- A: Study
- B: Attic
- C: Conservatory
- D: Kitchen

15

Which TV comedy series was
made famous by Rowan Atkinson?

- A: Blueviper
- B: Greensnake
- C: Redcobra
- D: Blackadder

50:50 Go to page 246   Go to page 258   ? Answers on page 267

6 ◆ £2,000

16

What name is given to one of
two equal parts of a whole?

- A: A third
- B: A fifth
- C: A tenth
- D: A half

17

Which original member of the
Spice Girls is called Geraldine?

- A: Baby Spice
- B: Ginger Spice
- C: Sporty Spice
- D: Scary Spice

18

What relation to you is the sister
of one of your parents?

- A: Grandmother
- B: Aunt
- C: Cousin
- D: Niece

19

Which of these plants can give a nasty sting?

- A: Thistle
- B: Rose
- C: Nettle
- D: Buttercup

20

What name is given to a ship
that can travel underwater?

- A: Aqua vessel
- B: Water sphere
- C: Marine tank
- D: Submarine

 **50:50** Go to page 246   Go to page 258   **?** Answers on page 267

6 ◆ £2,000

21

Who wanted to 'phone home' in the
1982 Stephen Spielberg film?

A: BT

B: ET

C: FT

D: NT

22

In films, what is the name of the
giant ape who terrorised New York?

A: Donkey Kong

B: Ding Dong

C: Ping Pong

D: King Kong

23

Which of these is a children's party race?

A: Dutch hoe

B: Watering can

C: Wheelbarrow

D: Hand trowel

24

What sort of pie is made with minced
meat and covered with mashed potatoes?

A: Fisherman's

B: Shepherd's

C: Blacksmith's

D: Fletcher's

25

Michael Owen plays for which football club?

A: Manchester United

B: Arsenal

C: Leeds United

D: Liverpool

50:50 Go to page 246   Go to page 258   ? Answers on page 267

6 ◆ £2,000

26

Who baptised Jesus?

A: Elijah the Prophet
B: Herod the Great
C: John the Baptist
D: Simon the Tax Collector

27

Which of these sports does not involve a ball?

A: Badminton
B: Tennis
C: Football
D: Golf

28

In whose 'Wild West Show' did Annie Oakley perform her trick shooting?

A: Buffalo Will's
B: Buffalo Bob's
C: Buffalo Bill's
D: Buffalo Rob's

29

What word describes the connected events running through a novel?

A: Blot
B: Slot
C: Plot
D: Clot

30

On which part of the body would a tiara be worn?

A: Feet
B: Legs
C: Hands
D: Head

50:50 Go to page 246   Go to page 258   ? Answers on page 267

6 ◆ £2,000

31

What is the second day of the week?

- A: Monday
- B: Tuesday
- C: Wednesday
- D: Thursday

32

In which building would grain be ground into flour?

- A: Mill
- B: Pottery
- C: Bakery
- D: Smithy

33

What name is given to a device for raising heavy objects off the ground?

- A: John
- B: Jack
- C: Sam
- D: Dave

34

Which punctuation mark indicates the end of a sentence?

- A: Comma
- B: Full stop
- C: Colon
- D: Inverted comma

35

What name was given to the English civil wars between the House of York and the House of Lancaster?

- A: Wars of the Irises
- B: Wars of the Roses
- C: Wars of the Daisies
- D: Wars of the Bluebells

50:50 Go to page 246  Go to page 258  Answers on page 267

6 ♦ £2,000

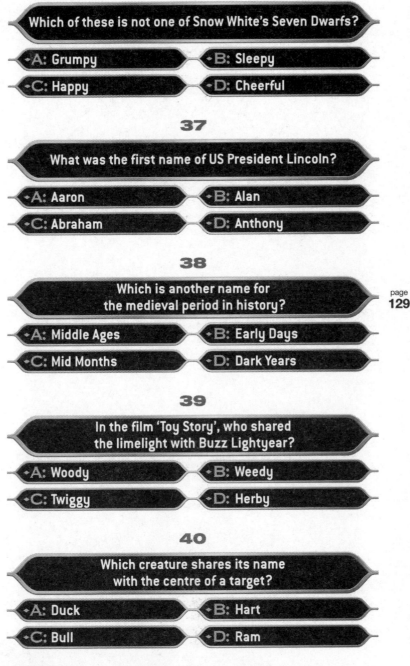

36

Which of these is not one of Snow White's Seven Dwarfs?

- A: Grumpy
- B: Sleepy
- C: Happy
- D: Cheerful

37

What was the first name of US President Lincoln?

- A: Aaron
- B: Alan
- C: Abraham
- D: Anthony

38

Which is another name for the medieval period in history?

- A: Middle Ages
- B: Early Days
- C: Mid Months
- D: Dark Years

page **129**

39

In the film 'Toy Story', who shared the limelight with Buzz Lightyear?

- A: Woody
- B: Weedy
- C: Twiggy
- D: Herby

40

Which creature shares its name with the centre of a target?

- A: Duck
- B: Hart
- C: Bull
- D: Ram

50:50 Go to page 246   Go to page 258   ? Answers on page 267

41

What is 12 x 11?

A: 99   B: 121

C: 110   D: 132

42

Which of these is a large metal container for rubbish?

A: Hop   B: Skip

C: Jump   D: Dive

43

What name is given to a sand pit on a golf course?

A: Bunker   B: Dunker

C: Munker   D: Punker

44

Which of these is a style of Chinese cooking?

A: Stir boil   B: Stir bake

C: Stir fry   D: Stir steam

45

What is the name of the horse in Anna Sewell's famous book?

A: Lilac Lovely   B: Purple Pretty

C: Brown Bonny   D: Black Beauty

50:50 Go to page 246   Go to page 258   ? Answers on page 267

6 ◆ £2,000

46

Which of these is a hugely successful TV puppet show?

A: The Moppets
B: The Muppets
C: The Poppets
D: The Puppets

47

Whose 'miniature world' is a popular toy?

A: Linda Lapel
B: Molly Mac
C: Polly Pocket
D: Claire Collar

48

Which organ pumps blood around the body?

A: Liver
B: Heart
C: Kidneys
D: Lungs

49

What name is given to the matching outfits worn on the playing field by football teams?

A: Strips
B: Streaks
C: Slips
D: Stripes

50

Which London structure, built to celebrate the new millennium, cost £750 million?

A: The Dome
B: The Bulge
C: The Hump
D: The Bump

50:50 Go to page 246   Go to page 258   ? Answers on page 267

6 ◆ £2,000

51

In Canada, what is most likely
to be eaten with pancakes?

A: Willow syrup

B: Elm syrup

C: Maple syrup

D: Oak syrup

52

Which word is associated with the sound of thunder?

A: Click

B: Clap

C: Clunk

D: Clang

53

What name is given to a small garment
which does not reach the waist?

A: Crop top

B: Spare top

C: Short top

D: Shrink top

54

Which of these is the title of
a hit song by Britney Spears?

A: Fun

B: Happy

C: Lucky

D: Treat

55

What is a series of six balls called in cricket?

A: Under

B: Over

C: End

D: Above

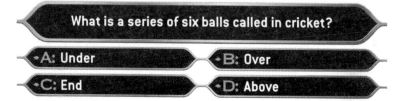
50:50 Go to page 246   Go to page 258   ? Answers on page 267

6 ◆ £2,000

56

Which TV cook is known as 'The Naked Chef'?

A: Delia Smith
B: Jamie Oliver
C: Ainsley Harriott
D: Gary Rhodes

57

Which telephone directory lists local businesses?

A: Red pages
B: Blue pages
C: Yellow pages
D: Grey pages

58

Which of these is a national daily UK newspaper?

A: Daily Letter
B: Daily Mail
C: Daily Chain
D: Daily Post

59

What is an unexpected and unfortunate event?

A: Act
B: Accident
C: Action
D: Access

60

In the Bible, who betrayed Jesus to the authorities?

A: Thomas
B: James
C: Judas
D: Matthew

 50:50 Go to page 246   Go to page 258   ? Answers on page 267

6 ◆ £2,000

61

Which of these is a type of shoe?

A: Coach
B: Trainer
C: Teacher
D: Mentor

62

How is the 'Professor' described in the title of the films starring Eddie Murphy?

A: Crackers
B: Nutty
C: Crazy
D: Cuckoo

63

Which of these is a radio soap?

A: The Archers
B: Hollyoaks
C: Emmerdale
D: Holby City

64

Where does the sun rise?

A: In the north
B: In the south
C: In the east
D: In the west

65

In the Bible, how many Commandments did God give to Moses?

A: 6
B: 8
C: 10
D: 12

50:50 Go to page 247   Go to page 258   ? Answers on page 267

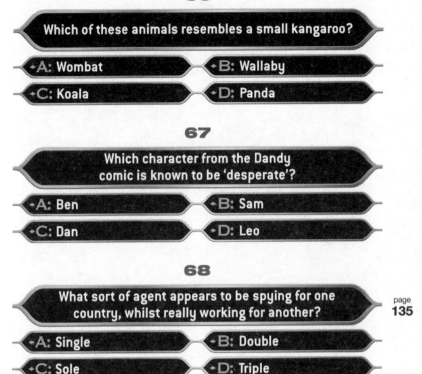

66

Which of these animals resembles a small kangaroo?

A: Wombat

B: Wallaby

C: Koala

D: Panda

67

Which character from the Dandy comic is known to be 'desperate'?

A: Ben

B: Sam

C: Dan

D: Leo

68

What sort of agent appears to be spying for one country, whilst really working for another?

A: Single

B: Double

C: Sole

D: Triple

page
135

15 **£1 MILLION**
14 £500,000
13 £250,000
12 £125,000
11 £64,000
10 **£32,000**
9 £16,000
8 £8,000

7 ◆ £4,000

6 ◆ £2,000
5 ◆ £1,000
4 ◆ £500
3 ◆ £300
2 ◆ £200
1 ◆ £100

7 ◆ £4,000

1

Which sort of ray can take a special photograph of the inside of a body?

A: W-ray

B: X-ray

C: Y-ray

D: Z-ray

2

The West Country is famous for which type of cream?

A: Clotted cream

B: Soured cream

C: Double cream

D: Single cream

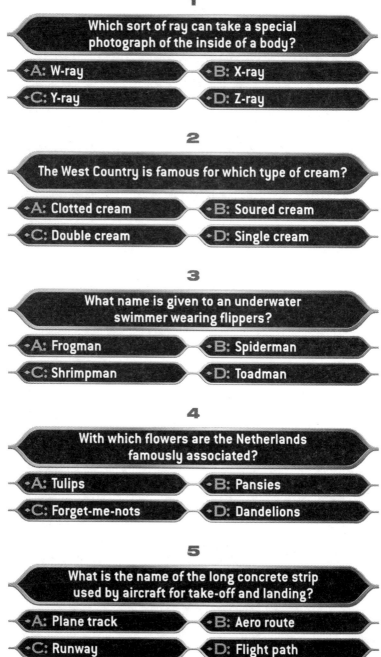

3

What name is given to an underwater swimmer wearing flippers?

A: Frogman

B: Spiderman

C: Shrimpman

D: Toadman

4

With which flowers are the Netherlands famously associated?

A: Tulips

B: Pansies

C: Forget-me-nots

D: Dandelions

5

What is the name of the long concrete strip used by aircraft for take-off and landing?

A: Plane track

B: Aero route

C: Runway

D: Flight path

50:50 Go to page 247   Go to page 259   **?** Answers on page 268

6

In which country is Florida?

- A: USA
- B: Australia
- C: Canada
- D: France

7

Which creature can be seen on the Welsh national flag?

- A: Red dragon
- B: Green lizard
- C: Blue snake
- D: Yellow snail

8

What did the Emperor Hadrian build to mark the northern border of Roman Britain?

- A: Moat
- B: Hedge
- C: Wall
- D: Fence

9

Which of these is the underwater link between England and France?

- A: Channel Tunnel
- B: Channel Funnel
- C: Channel Passage
- D: Channel Gate

10

Where in the body are the biceps?

- A: Arm
- B: Leg
- C: Hand
- D: Foot

50:50 Go to page 247   Go to page 259   ❓ Answers on page 268

11

Which sea is off the east coast of Great Britain?

◆A: South Sea ◆B: East Sea

◆C: West Sea ◆D: North Sea

12

What is the name of Punch and Judy's dog?

◆A: Harry ◆B: Sam

◆C: Andy ◆D: Toby

13

Which part of the country lies between the north and south of England?

◆A: The Lowlands ◆B: The Highlands

◆C: The Midlands ◆D: The Uplands

14

Who are the 'little people' of Ireland?

◆A: Sprites ◆B: Gremlins

◆C: Pixies ◆D: Leprechauns

15

Which of these is a former Prime Minister of the UK?

◆A: John Captain ◆B: John Corporal

◆C: John Major ◆D: John General

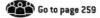

50:50 Go to page 247   Go to page 259   **?** Answers on page 268

16

What is a one-wheeled cycle called?

- A: Unicycle
- B: Bicycle
- C: Tricycle
- D: Moped

17

Which expression means 'turned over', so the bottom is at the top?

- A: Upside-down
- B: Inside-out
- C: Back to front
- D: Round and round

18

What is the name of the friendly green ogre in the 2001 animated feature film?

- A: Shrek
- B: Shriek
- C: Shiek
- D: Shred

19

Which word means a conspicuous or well known object on land?

- A: Landscape
- B: Landmark
- C: Landslide
- D: Landlord

20

Wimbledon is a famous venue for which sport?

- A: Tennis
- B: Golf
- C: Horse racing
- D: Hockey

50:50 Go to page 247   Go to page 259   ? Answers on page 268

7 ◆ £4,000

21

Which of these is a small breed
of dog with a flattened snout?

- A: Bug
- B: Mug
- C: Pug
- D: Lug

22

Whose name will be forever linked with a snack food?

- A: Earl of Sandwich
- B: Duke of Biscuit
- C: Crown Prince Butty
- D: Count Crisp

23

Which of the following is a bird?

- A: Swallow
- B: Gargle
- C: Gulp
- D: Choke

24

What name is given to a long speech by one person?

- A: Monopoly
- B: Monotonous
- C: Monologue
- D: Monsoon

25

Which bird shares its name with an edible fruit?

- A: Pawpaw
- B: Kiwi
- C: Mango
- D: Banana

50:50 Go to page 247   Go to page 259   ? Answers on page 268

7 ◆ £4,000

26

What name is given to a building where things are made by machines?

A: Factory

B: Warehouse

C: Stadium

D: Office

27

Which TV soap is set in Australia?

A: EastEnders

B: Coronation Street

C: Emmerdale

D: Neighbours

28

What is a room said to be when microphones have been secretly installed?

A: Dogged

B: Wormed

C: Bugged

D: Loused

29

In which country is bullfighting a popular event?

A: England

B: Norway

C: Spain

D: Greece

30

'Architect' comes from the Greek for which word?

A: Baker

B: Builder

C: Boxer

D: Bowler

50:50 Go to page 247   Go to page 259   ? Answers on page 268

7 ◆ £4,000

31

Which of these is not an anagram of POST?

- A: Spot
- B: Tops
- C: Stop
- D: Step

32

What sort of musical instrument is shaped like a cauldron and sits on three legs?

- A: Kettledrum
- B: Irondrum
- C: Toasterdrum
- D: Dryerdrum

33

Which expression means 'everything is perfect'?

- A: Bob a job
- B: Bits and bobs
- C: Bob the Builder
- D: Bob's your uncle

34

Mutton is meat from which animal?

- A: Cow
- B: Pig
- C: Sheep
- D: Deer

35

In which of these would you find a joker?

- A: Chess
- B: Backgammon
- C: Cards
- D: Marbles

50:50 Go to page 247  Go to page 259  Answers on page 268

36

According to the legend, who slew a dragon?

A: St David

B: St Andrew

C: St George

D: St Patrick

37

What name was given to a man who fought on horseback in olden times?

A: Page

B: Squire

C: Serf

D: Knight

38

Which of these was a famous Roman general and statesman?

A: Julius Caesar

B: John Cabot

C: Captain Cook

D: Charles I

39

Natural paper is obtained from which source?

A: Trees

B: Oil

C: Rock

D: Shell

40

Which animals' feet are called 'trotters'?

A: Cows

B: Pigs

C: Sheep

D: Deer

41

Of what was the wicked witch's house made, in the fairy story 'Hansel and Gretel'?

A: Marzipan
B: Doughnuts
C: Gingerbread
D: Chocolate gateau

42

Which silent film star was famous for his role as a baggy-trousered tramp?

A: Charlie Chaplin
B: Freddy Chaplin
C: Sammy Chaplin
D: Harry Chaplin

43

How many books are there in a trilogy?

A: 1
B: 2
C: 3
D: 4

44

Which conquest of England took place in 1066?

A: Albert
B: Norman
C: Stanley
D: Edgar

45

Who was 'the spy' in the 1996 film of the same name?

A: Hannah
B: Harriet
C: Helen
D: Holly

 50:50 Go to page 247   Go to page 259    ? Answers on page 268

7 ◆ £4,000

46

Which of these is a senior member of the Roman Catholic church?

- A: Bishop
- B: Castle
- C: King
- D: Rook

47

What is the French word for 'sweets'?

- A: Bonbons
- B: Dondons
- C: Sonsons
- D: Tontons

48

Which is a male goose?

- A: Gander
- B: Dander
- C: Fender
- D: Gender

49

What name is given to a famous arch in London?

- A: Granite Arch
- B: Stone Arch
- C: Marble Arch
- D: Slate Arch

50

Which Kate is a supermodel?

- A: Bush
- B: Fern
- C: Moss
- D: Tree

50:50 Go to page 247   Go to page 259   **?** Answers on page 268

7 ◆ £4,000

51

What sort of words are 'doing' words?

- A: Verbs
- B: Nouns
- C: Adjectives
- D: Adverbs

52

Which word is used when speaking to a king or queen?

- A: Holiness
- B: Honour
- C: Majesty
- D: Lord

53

What name is given to someone who makes furniture out of wood?

- A: Joiner
- B: Fastener
- C: Holder
- D: Fixer

54

Which of these is the title of a book by Mary Norton, about a family of tiny people?

- A: The Lenders
- B: The Borrowers
- C: The Hirers
- D: The Renters

55

Which of the following is the name of a London international airport?

- A: Heathrow
- B: Westminster
- C: Paddington
- D: Windsor

50:50 Go to page 247   Go to page 259   ? Answers on page 268

7 ◆ £4,000

56

Which of these is not a musical instrument?

A: Violin

B: Viola

C: Violet

D: Double Bass

57

What name is given to a long wooden seat in a church?

A: Pew

B: Hew

C: Dew

D: Few

58

Which day is celebrated on February 14th?

A: Christmas Day

B: Boxing Day

C: St Valentine's Day

D: Pancake Day

59

What was the 'Starlight Express' in Andrew Lloyd Webber's musical of the same name?

A: Boat

B: Train

C: Plane

D: Car

60

In which type of restaurant might you order 'Sweet and Sour Pork'?

A: Indian

B: French

C: Chinese

D: English

50:50 Go to page 247   Go to page 259   Answers on page 268

7 ◆ £4,000

61

Complete this James Bond
film title: 'The World is Not...'?

A: Round

B: Flat

C: Enough

D: Safe

62

Which of these is a BBC TV documentary series
of 2001, narrated by Sir David Attenborough?

A: Green Planet

B: Red Planet

C: Grey Planet

D: Blue Planet

63

On TV, how are Milo, Jake, Fizz and Bella better known?

A: The Tweenies

B: The Tinies

C: The Tweeties

D: The Sweeties

64

Which entertainer is associated with
the TV programme 'Animal Hospital'?

A: Anthea Turner

B: Johnny Vaughan

C: Rolf Harris

D: Kylie Minogue

 50:50 Go to page 247   Go to page 259    ? Answers on page 268

15	**£1 MILLION**
14	£500,000
13	£250,000
12	£125,000
11	£64,000
10	**£32,000**
9	£16,000
8 ◆	**£8,000**
7 ◆	£4,000
6 ◆	£2,000
5 ◆	£1,000
4 ◆	£500
3 ◆	£300
2 ◆	£200
1 ◆	£100

8 ◆ £8,000

1

Which of the following is a type of clock, commonly made in Switzerland?

- A: Magpie
- B: Sparrow
- C: Cuckoo
- D: Eagle

2

What sort of fruit is a sultana?

- A: Dried plum
- B: Dried grape
- C: Dried apricot
- D: Dried cherry

3

In which comic does the character Dennis the Menace appear?

- A: Beano
- B: Dandy
- C: Hotspur
- D: Spiderman

4

In the nursery rhyme, what did Old King Cole call for first?

- A: Bowl
- B: Pipe
- C: Fiddlers
- D: Wife

5

Which police squad has special training enabling them to respond rapidly to the scene of a crime?

- A: Flying squad
- B: Sitting squad
- C: Standing squad
- D: Walking squad

50:50 Go to page 248   Go to page 260   ? Answers on page 268

8 ◆ £8,000

6

According to the proverb, what should you let sleeping dogs do?

A: Sleep | B: Lie
C: Sit | D: Slouch

7

Which is a national emblem of England?

A: Bluebell | B: Snowdrop
C: Iris | D: Rose

8

What is the surname of 'Buffy - The Vampire Slayer'?

A: Springs | B: Autumns
C: Summers | D: Winters

9

Which of these is not a citrus fruit?

A: Lemon | B: Lime
C: Apple | D: Orange

10

Where in the world do polar bears live?

A: Africa | B: Arctic
C: Australia | D: Antarctic

50:50 Go to page 248   Go to page 260   Answers on page 268

8 ◆ £8,000

11

From which tree are conkers obtained?

- A: Horse chestnut
- B: Oak
- C: Lime
- D: Beech

12

Tony Blair, the British Prime Minister, is the leader of which political party?

- A: Conservative
- B: Liberal Democrat
- C: Labour
- D: Scottish Nationalist

13

Which of these is a flying mammal?

- A: Hoop
- B: Puck
- C: Bat
- D: Stump

14

Who was the love of Tarzan's life?

- A: Mary
- B: Jane
- C: Susan
- D: Sarah

15

Which plague killed millions of people in the 14th century?

- A: Red Death
- B: Black Death
- C: Blue Death
- D: Yellow Death

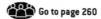 50:50 Go to page 248    Go to page 260   ? Answers on page 268

8 ◆ £8,000

16

What name is given to the stretch of
water between England and France?

- A: English Sea
- B: English Channel
- C: English Straits
- D: English Flows

17

Which of these is a famous landmark
in the town of Blackpool?

- A: Castle
- B: Cathedral
- C: Palace
- D: Tower

18

How many thieves were there in the folk tale 'Ali Baba'?

- A: 20
- B: 40
- C: 60
- D: 80

19

Which of these is an edible nut?

- A: Argentina
- B: Peru
- C: Brazil
- D: Mexico

20

What name is given to a piece of wire worn
across the teeth to straighten them?

- A: Hook
- B: Brace
- C: Link
- D: Clamp

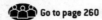 50:50 Go to page 248   Go to page 260   ? Answers on page 268

8 ◆ £8,000

21

Which of these is a famous professional golfer?

A: Lion Brown

B: Tiger Woods

C: Puma Smith

D: Cheetah Grey

22

According to the TV advertisement, when you 'have a break' what should you eat?

A: Milky Way

B: Smarties

C: Kit Kat

D: Mars bar

23

Which of these would be found in an orchestra?

A: Square

B: Rectangle

C: Circle

D: Triangle

24

What name is given to the body of a ship?

A: York

B: Leeds

C: Hull

D: Wick

25

Traditionally which material is used in the manufacture of jeans?

A: Silk

B: Denim

C: Wool

D: Leather

50:50 Go to page 248   Go to page 260   ? Answers on page 268

26

Richard Whiteley presents which Channel 4 quiz show?

◆A: Countdown
◆B: Add Up
◆C: Take Away
◆D: Divide

27

In tennis, what name is given to the winning of all four major tournaments in one season?

◆A: Triple crown
◆B: Grand slam
◆C: Ashes
◆D: Yellow jersey

28

'The Sheep-Pig', written by Dick King-Smith, was made into which popular film?

◆A: Piglet
◆B: Wilbur
◆C: Miss Piggy
◆D: Babe

29

How many letters are there in the English alphabet?

◆A: 20
◆B: 26
◆C: 30
◆D: 36

30

Which of the following is a famous British horse race?

◆A: Great National
◆B: Grand National
◆C: Big National
◆D: Super National

50:50 Go to page 248   Go to page 260   Answers on page 268

8 ◆ £8,000

31

What was the first name of the German dictator Hitler?

A: Hans

B: Ludwig

C: Adolf

D: Heinrich

32

Which word means 'to draw or scribble meaninglessly'?

A: Boodle

B: Doodle

C: Poodle

D: Noodle

33

Complete the expression, 'Mad as a...'

A: March hare

B: January cat

C: May bug

D: April fool

34

Which Italian adventurer shares his last name with a popular sweet?

A: Marco Smarties

B: Marco Polo

C: Marco Smint

D: Marco Twix

35

In football, what name is given to a player in an attacking position whose main role is to score goals?

A: Hitter

B: Striker

C: Beater

D: Thumper

50:50 Go to page 248   Go to page 260   Answers on page 268

8 ◆ £8,000

36

Which creature gives us silk thread?

A: Silky bear
B: Silk snake
C: Silkworm
D: Silky chimpanzee

37

How is the giant observation wheel in London otherwise known?

A: The London Eye
B: The London Nose
C: The London Ear
D: The London Mouth

38

In which month is Hallowe'en celebrated?

A: September
B: October
C: November
D: December

39

Maggie, Meg and Peggy are all short versions of which name?

A: Susan
B: Mary
C: Margaret
D: Victoria

40

Which is the fastest land animal?

A: Ostrich
B: Cheetah
C: Lion
D: Giraffe

 50:50 Go to page 248   Go to page 260    ? Answers on page 268

8 ◆ £8,000

41

How many players are there in a hockey team?

A: 7
B: 9
C: 11
D: 15

42

What does the prefix 'milli' mean, as in the word millimetre?

A: 1 tenth
B: 1 hundredth
C: 1 millionth
D: 1 thousandth

43

Which of these is not a natural product?

A: Wool
B: Cotton
C: Nylon
D: Silk

44

Who partners Dr Jekyll when describing someone who has both a good and a bad personality?

A: Mr Hyde
B: Mr Seek
C: Mr Cloak
D: Mr Dagger

45

Which of these is another name for a violin?

A: Sham
B: Spoof
C: Bluff
D: Fiddle

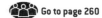 50:50 Go to page 248   Go to page 260    Answers on page 268

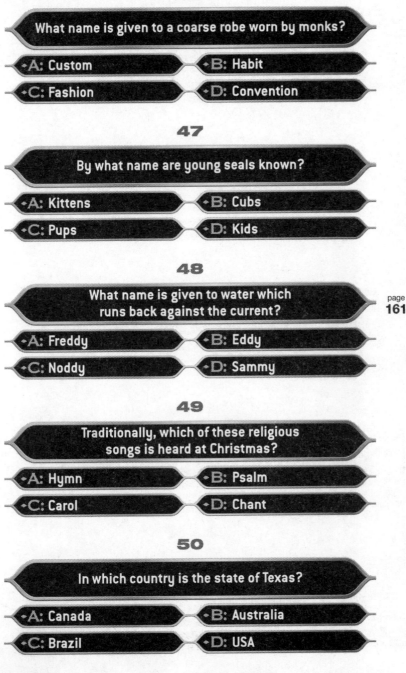

46

What name is given to a coarse robe worn by monks?

- A: Custom
- B: Habit
- C: Fashion
- D: Convention

47

By what name are young seals known?

- A: Kittens
- B: Cubs
- C: Pups
- D: Kids

48

What name is given to water which runs back against the current?

- A: Freddy
- B: Eddy
- C: Noddy
- D: Sammy

49

Traditionally, which of these religious songs is heard at Christmas?

- A: Hymn
- B: Psalm
- C: Carol
- D: Chant

50

In which country is the state of Texas?

- A: Canada
- B: Australia
- C: Brazil
- D: USA

50:50 Go to page 248   Go to page 260   ? Answers on page 268

8 ◆ £8,000

51

What sort of troops are the infantry?

A: Foot soldiers

B: Arm soldiers

C: Leg soldiers

D: Hand soldiers

52

Which of these means 'not transparent'?

A: Opal

B: Opaque

C: Oppose

D: Optical

53

Approximately when do Christians believe Jesus Christ was born?

A: 2000 years ago

B: 1000 years ago

C: 500 years ago

D: 100 years ago

54

At what age can one legally leave school in the UK?

A: 15

B: 16

C: 17

D: 18

55

Croissants are usually eaten at which meal?

A: Breakfast

B: Lunch

C: Afternoon tea

D: Dinner

50:50 Go to page 248  Go to page 260  **?** Answers on page 268

8 ◆ £8,000

56

What is the name of the extra large Beanie Babies?

A: Biggies
B: Buddies
C: Baggies
D: Buggies

57

Lois Lane is the girlfriend of which super hero?

A: Spiderman
B: Superman
C: Batman
D: Action Man

58

In the adventure story 'Treasure Island', what did the pirate Long John Silver have on his shoulder?

page 163

A: A bag
B: A parrot
C: A rifle
D: A telescope

59

'All Rise' was the Christmas 2001 album by which boy band?

A: Red
B: Yellow
C: Blue
D: Green

60

Name the film series starring Peter Sellers as Inspector Clouseau.

A: Pink Panther
B: Lime Leopard
C: Chocolate Cheetah
D: Lemon Lion

50:50 Go to page 248   Go to page 260   ? Answers on page 268

50:50		

15   £1 MILLION

14   £500,000

13   £250,000

12   £125,000

11   £64,000

10   £32,000

9 ◆ £16,000

8 ◆ £8,000

7 ◆ £4,000

6 ◆ £2,000

5 ◆ £1,000

4 ◆ £500

3 ◆ £300

2 ◆ £200

1 ◆ £100

9 ◆ £16,000

1

Which 'family' includes the members
Gomez, Morticia and Uncle Fester?

- A: Partridge
- B: Monkees
- C: Addams
- D: Cartwright

2

What is the Sahara?

- A: Desert
- B: River
- C: Mountain
- D: Sea

3

Which of these is an insect similar to a grasshopper?

- A: Football
- B: Cricket
- C: Golf
- D: Rounders

4

In which wood do Winnie-the-Pooh and his friends live?

- A: Hundred Acre Wood
- B: Two Hundred Acre Wood
- C: Three Hundred Acre Wood
- D: Four Hundred Acre Wood

5

What does the crocodile swallow
in the story of Peter Pan?

- A: Toothbrush
- B: Clock
- C: Radio
- D: Hairbrush

50:50 Go to page 248 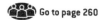 Go to page 260  Answers on page 268

9 ◆ £16,000

6

Which of the following is used to steer a boat?

A: Rudder
B: Hull
C: Keel
D: Anchor

7

In how many states does water exist?

A: 1
B: 2
C: 3
D: 4

8

Which of these is not a primary painting colour?

A: Red
B: Blue
C: Yellow
D: Purple

9

How many strings has a cello?

A: 4
B: 5
C: 6
D: 7

10

Which of these flowers is not yellow?

A: Buttercup
B: Primrose
C: Snowdrop
D: Celandine

 50:50 Go to page 248   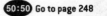 Go to page 260    **?** Answers on page 268

9 ◆ £16,000

11

In the board game Monopoly, what is the most valuable property?

A: Park Lane

B: Mayfair

C: Fleet Street

D: The Water Works

12

Which of these is a garment worn by the ancient Romans?

A: Kimono

B: Sari

C: Toga

D: Sarong

13

What was given back to China in 1997?

A: Mah Jong

B: Ping Pong

C: Hong Kong

D: Sing Song

14

Which painted pole do people traditionally dance around whilst holding ribbons?

A: Marchpole

B: Maypole

C: Junepole

D: Julypole

15

What sort of creature is a whale?

A: Reptile

B: Mammal

C: Fish

D: Amphibian

50:50 Go to page 248   Go to page 260   ? Answers on page 268

9 ◆ £16,000

16

In which section of the orchestra are the drums and cymbals?

- A: Woodwind
- B: Brass
- C: Percussion
- D: Strings

17

Which of these is a scientific instrument for magnifying small objects?

- A: Horoscope
- B: Telescope
- C: Periscope
- D: Microscope

18

What is pressed in a car to make it go faster?

- A: Clutch
- B: Brake
- C: Horn
- D: Accelerator

19

Which is the only continent where giraffes are found in the wild?

- A: Asia
- B: Europe
- C: Africa
- D: North America

20

Oranges are rich in which vitamin?

- A: A
- B: C
- C: D
- D: E

50:50 Go to page 248 Go to page 261 **?** Answers on page 268

9 ◆ £16,000

21

Which of these is a form of Japanese wrestling?

A: Sumo

B: Sake

C: Take

D: Sushi

22

Jack O'Neill, Teal'c and Samantha Carter are characters in which science fiction TV series?

A: Dr Who

B: Star Trek

C: Stargate SG 1

D: Farscape

23

Which of these is a character from the Charles Dickens short story 'A Christmas Carol'?

A: Scrooge

B: Scrimp

C: Scrounge

D: Squander

24

What name is given to the area next to the ear above the cheekbone?

A: Church

B: Temple

C: Chapel

D: Mosque

25

Which of these is not one of the five senses?

A: Blink

B: Touch

C: Smell

D: Sight

50:50 Go to page 249   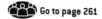 Go to page 261   ❓  Answers on page 268

9 ◆ £16,000

26

The Roman god Mars gave his name to which month?

- ◆ A: May
- ◆ B: April
- ◆ C: March
- ◆ D: June

27

Which of these means 'situated in or belonging to a town or city'?

- ◆ A: Urban
- ◆ B: Rural
- ◆ C: Pastoral
- ◆ D: Coastal

28

Complete this phrase: 'The White Cliffs of...'?

- ◆ A: Southampton
- ◆ B: Plymouth
- ◆ C: Dover
- ◆ D: Brighton

29

Which of these is a wild dog of Australia?

- ◆ A: Bongo
- ◆ B: Kango
- ◆ C: Pongo
- ◆ D: Dingo

30

How many legs has a spider?

- ◆ A: 2
- ◆ B: 4
- ◆ C: 6
- ◆ D: 8

50:50 Go to page 249   Go to page 261   ? Answers on page 268

9 ◆ £16,000

31

Which of these words does not mean 'very small'?

- A: Tiny
- B: Minute
- C: Speck
- D: Mass

32

Which imaginary land is visited while asleep?

- A: Forty winks
- B: Sleep city
- C: The Land of Nod
- D: Neverland

33

Who is the patron saint of Ireland?

- A: St George
- B: St Andrew
- C: St Patrick
- D: St David

34

Which salad dressing is made from oil, spices and lemon juice or vinegar?

- A: Spanish
- B: German
- C: French
- D: English

35

Which of these is not a vowel?

- A: A
- B: C
- C: E
- D: O

50:50 Go to page 249   Go to page 261   **?** Answers on page 268

9 ◆ £16,000

36

By what name is the American
national flag commonly known?

- A: Stars and Stripes
- B: Squares and Stripes
- C: Suns and Stripes
- D: Moons and Stripes

37

Which of these winds is the strongest?

- A: Breeze
- B: Storm
- C: Gale
- D: Hurricane

38

What name is given to the illusions
often experienced in a desert?

page
173

- A: Mirror
- B: Miracle
- C: Mirage
- D: Mire

39

Which is the small, thin piece of skin
inside the ear which transmits vibrations?

- A: Eardrum
- B: Earlobe
- C: Earpiece
- D: Earring

40

Which of these is an organisation
dedicated to saving the planet Earth?

- A: Greenfingers
- B: Greenpeace
- C: Greenhouse
- D: Greengage

 50:50 Go to page 249   Go to page 261    ? Answers on page 268

41

In the story of Cinderella, which animals were magically transformed into horses for the carriage?

- A: Rats
- B: Rabbits
- C: Mice
- D: Stoats

42

Which Walt Disney cartoon character first appeared in 1928?

- A: Danger Mouse
- B: Mickey Mouse
- C: Mighty Mouse
- D: Jerry Mouse

43

Which bird lays the largest eggs?

- A: Golden Eagle
- B: Penguin
- C: Ostrich
- D: Vulture

44

In the 'William' stories by Richmal Crompton, what is his last name?

- A: Blue
- B: Brown
- C: Black
- D: Green

45

Which of these words means to eat greedily?

- A: Gibber
- B: Gobble
- C: Gabble
- D: Mumble

50:50 Go to page 249   Go to page 261   ? Answers on page 268

9 ◆ £16,000

46

Which is a short prayer said before or after a meal?

◆A: Grace
◆B: Faith
◆C: Joy
◆D: Gaye

47

'Great rats, small rats, lean rats, brawny rats' is a line from which famous poem?

◆A: The Owl and the Pussycat
◆B: The Pied Piper of Hamelin
◆C: Matilda
◆D: Jabberwocky

48

Which punctuation mark is used to join parts of words together?

page
175

◆A: Colon
◆B: Hyphen
◆C: Comma
◆D: Full stop

49

Which of these is a famous John Travolta dance movie?

◆A: Sunday Night Shivers
◆B: Saturday Night Fever
◆C: Tuesday Night Toothache
◆D: Monday Night Migraine

50

What colour is a piebald horse?

◆A: Brown and white
◆B: Black and white
◆C: Brown
◆D: Black

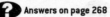 **50:50** Go to page 249   **Go to page 261**   **?** Answers on page 268

9 ♦ £16,000

51

Which unusual fashion accessory was worn by pop vocalist Gabrielle?

- A: Headband
- B: Sling
- C: Choker
- D: Eyepatch

52

Which TV personality hosts 'Blind Date'?

- A: Carol Vorderman
- B: Anthea Turner
- C: Cilla Black
- D: Lorraine Kelly

53

What does the word 'advent' mean as in the religious period just before Christmas?

- A: Coming
- B: Calendar
- C: Christmas
- D: Crackers

54

Which product is advertised on TV by the ex-footballer Gary Lineker?

- A: Coca-Cola
- B: Mars bars
- C: 7 UP
- D: Walker's crisps

55

In which city would you find Red Square?

- A: Moscow
- B: Paris
- C: Rome
- D: Madrid

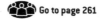 50:50 Go to page 249   Go to page 261    Answers on page 268

56

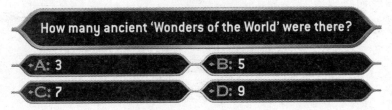

How many ancient 'Wonders of the World' were there?

A: 3

B: 5

C: 7

D: 9

15	**£1 MILLION**
14	£500,000
13	£250,000
12	£125,000
11	£64,000
10 ◆	**£32,000**
9 ◆	£16,000
8 ◆	£8,000
7 ◆	£4,000
6 ◆	£2,000
5 ◆	**£1,000**
4 ◆	£500
3 ◆	£300
2 ◆	£200
1 ◆	£100

10 ◆ £32,000

1

Which profession do you associate with Fleet Street?

- A: Law
- B: Medicine
- C: Police
- D: Journalism

2

In the strip cartoon 'Dennis the Menace', what is the name of Gnasher's son?

- A: Gladdie
- B: Gsonny
- C: Gnipper
- D: Gkiddie

3

How many colours are there in a rainbow?

- A: 3
- B: 5
- C: 7
- D: 9

4

Which animal is stamped on British eggs as a sign of quality control?

- A: Lion
- B: Bear
- C: Dog
- D: Kangaroo

5

On which river does the city of Bristol stand?

- A: Avon
- B: Trent
- C: Thames
- D: Mersey

50:50 Go to page 249   Go to page 261   ? Answers on page 269

6

Traditionally, what colour are London taxis?

A: Black   B: Blue

C: Yellow   D: Red

7

Which geometric shape has four equal sides and four right angles?

A: Square   B: Triangle

C: Rhombus   D: Trapezium

8

Who married the Owl and Pussycat in the poem by Edward Lear?

A: Goose   B: Turkey

C: Chicken   D: Duck

9

Which ocean separates the UK from the USA?

A: Pacific   B: Atlantic

C: Indian   D: Arctic

10

In the book 'Charlotte's Web', what did Charlotte first write in her web about her friend Wilbur?

A: 'Some horse'   B: 'Some dog'

C: 'Some pig'   D: 'Some cat'

50:50 Go to page 249   Go to page 261   ? Answers on page 269

10 ◆ £32,000

11

Which of the following is a straight line between two places?

- A: Beeline
- B: Wasp-line
- C: Beetle-line
- D: Dragonfly-line

12

What can you see in a planetarium?

- A: Images of planets
- B: Images of plans
- C: Images of planes
- D: Images of plants

13

Which member of the Royal family celebrated their 100th birthday in August 2000?

- A: Queen Mother
- B: Princess Margaret
- C: Duke of Edinburgh
- D: Duke of Kent

14

What can be seen at Lord's in London on a summer's day?

- A: Cricket
- B: Boating
- C: Horse riding
- D: Open air concert

15

In which city is Cadbury World?

- A: London
- B: Manchester
- C: Bristol
- D: Birmingham

50:50 Go to page 249   Go to page 261   ? Answers on page 269

10 ◆ £32,000

16

When was the Battle of Hastings?

A: 1066
B: 1466
C: 1666
D: 1966

17

Which of these is a small poisonous snake?

A: Ruler
B: Adder
C: Divisor
D: Satchel

18

How is TV's 'Warrior Princess' better known?

A: Zara
B: Xena
C: Sara
D: Beta

19

In which century are we now living?

A: 18th
B: 19th
C: 20th
D: 21st

20

What name is given to the enclosed areas on canals where the water level can be changed?

A: Locks
B: Quays
C: Bolts
D: Catches

50:50 Go to page 249   Go to page 261   ? Answers on page 269

10 ◆ £32,000

21

Which country is the largest in the UK?

- A: England
- B: Scotland
- C: Wales
- D: Northern Ireland

22

What was Pablo Picasso's profession?

- A: Dancer
- B: Artist
- C: Musician
- D: Writer

23

Which 'Florence' was the founder of modern nursing?

- A: Sparrow
- B: Nightingale
- C: Robin
- D: Lark

24

Where would you find 'catkins'?

- A: In the road
- B: Under water
- C: In a cattery
- D: On a tree

25

Which of these words is used to describe meat with no fat?

- A: Thin
- B: Lank
- C: Lean
- D: Gaunt

 50:50 Go to page 249   Go to page 261   ? Answers on page 269

10 ◆ £32,000

26

In science, which type of paper is turned red by an acid and blue by an alkali?

- A: Litmus paper
- B: Wrapping paper
- C: Rice paper
- D: Blotting paper

27

How many players are there in a netball team?

- A: 5
- B: 7
- C: 9
- D: 11

28

Which type of film story deals with imaginative technological events, often set in the future?

page 185

- A: Horror
- B: Science fiction
- C: Costume drama
- D: Documentary

29

When the weather is very bad, what is it said to be raining?

- A: Rats and bats
- B: Cats and dogs
- C: Rabbits and hares
- D: Newts and toads

30

Which of these is a song supposedly written by King Henry VIII?

- A: Blue stockings
- B: Greensleeves
- C: Red slippers
- D: Yellow berets

 50:50 Go to page 249   Go to page 261   Answers on page 269

10 ◆ £32,000

31

What was Joan of Arc accused of, that led to her being burned at the stake?

A: Treason
B: Witchcraft
C: Murder
D: Spying

32

Which ballerina had a meringue pie named after her?

A: Anna Pavlova
B: Isadora Duncan
C: Josephine Baker
D: Margot Fonteyn

33

With which sport is Lester Piggott most famously associated?

A: Motor racing
B: Horse-racing
C: Tennis
D: Golf

34

How many years apart are the summer Olympic Games celebrated?

A: 2
B: 4
C: 6
D: 8

35

Which of these words is French for yellow?

A: Rose
B: Jaune
C: Gris
D: Bleu

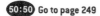 50:50 Go to page 249    Go to page 261    Answers on page 269

10 ◆ £32,000

36

What is the official currency of Australia?

A: Pound
B: Dollar
C: Penny
D: Franc

37

For which detail is the famous painting,
the Mona Lisa, best known?

A: Her hair
B: Her smile
C: Her teeth
D: Her jewellery

38

What name is given to young fish?

A: Grill
B: Broil
C: Mash
D: Fry

39

Which famous book was compiled for
William the Conqueror in 1085?

A: Magna Carta
B: Domesday
C: Book of Kells
D: Bill of Rights

40

What name is given to a list of computer
functions displayed on a screen?

A: Network
B: Menu
C: Hardware
D: Maindrive

50:50 Go to page 249   Go to page 261   ? Answers on page 269

10 ◆ £32,000

41

In which country is the White House the official residence of the president?

◆A: Canada
◆B: USA
◆C: Australia
◆D: New Zealand

42

For what is H_2O the chemical formula?

◆A: Water
◆B: Lemonade
◆C: Milk
◆D: Tea

43

Which of these is a Jewish place of worship?

◆A: Chapel
◆B: Mosque
◆C: Cathedral
◆D: Synagogue

44

Amongst these characters from 'The Lord of the Rings', who is the wizard?

◆A: Frodo Baggins
◆B: Gandalf
◆C: Samwise Gamgee
◆D: Peregrine Took

45

Which pop star shares a name with a character in 'Scooby Doo'?

◆A: Fred
◆B: Daphne
◆C: Shaggy
◆D: Velma

50:50 Go to page 250   Go to page 262   ? Answers on page 269

46

Which pickled vegetable is often served in a McDonald's hamburger?

A: Gherkin

B: Onion

C: Corn

D: Pepper

47

In Joan Aitken's book, which animals prowl around Willoughby Chase?

A: Tigers

B: Dogs

C: Cats

D: Wolves

48

Gammon is cured meat from which animal?

A: Deer

B: Cow

C: Pig

D: Sheep

49

Oprah Winfrey is a famous American TV what?

A: Doctor

B: Talk-show host

C: Gardener

D: Newsreader

50

Which of these is a WWF wrestler?

A: FFF

B: GGG

C: HHH

D: JJJ

51

Why is the chameleon a remarkable lizard?

- A: Never closes its eyes
- B: Eats only once a month
- C: Can change colour
- D: Can swim long distances

52

Which 'Challenge' is a TV quiz programme presented by Jeremy Paxman?

- A: College
- B: Tertiary
- C: Sixth Form
- D: University

50:50 Go to page 250  Go to page 262  Answers on page 269

50:50		

15   **£1 MILLION**

14   £500,000

13   £250,000

12   £125,000

11 ◆ £64,000

10 ◆ £32,000

9 ◆ £16,000

8 ◆ £8,000

7 ◆ £4,000

6 ◆ £2,000

5 ◆ £1,000

4 ◆ £500

3 ◆ £300

2 ◆ £200

1 ◆ £100

1

Which of these is a famous bicycle race?

A: Tour de Britain
B: Tour de France
C: Tour de Germany
D: Tour de Canada

2

By what name are the little boats that tow ships into port known?

A: Pulls
B: Tugs
C: Yanks
D: Pushes

3

Which is the capital city of Wales?

A: Wrexham
B: Swansea
C: Cardiff
D: Aberystwyth

4

What is the name of the only supersonic airliner in the world?

A: Concorde
B: Concourse
C: Console
D: Camcord

5

Which sport is a traditional Irish game resembling hockey?

A: Hurling
B: Furling
C: Swirling
D: Curling

50:50 Go to page 250   Go to page 262   Answers on page 269

11 ◆ £64,000

6

What was Horatio Nelson's most famous battle?

- A: Waterloo
- B: Britain
- C: Trafalgar
- D: Hastings

7

Which is the largest ocean on earth?

- A: Arctic
- B: Atlantic
- C: Pacific
- D: Indian

8

What name is given to the part of a bird's body at the base of the back?

- A: Rump
- B: Lump
- C: Bump
- D: Hump

9

To which royal house does Queen Elizabeth II belong?

- A: Hanover
- B: Stuart
- C: Windsor
- D: York

10

What word is used to describe trees that are 'in leaf' throughout the year?

- A: Deciduous
- B: Coniferous
- C: Evergreen
- D: Arboreal

50:50 Go to page 250   Go to page 262   Answers on page 269

11

Which of these is not a type of pasta?

A: Spaghetti

B: Macaroni

C: Basmati

D: Ravioli

12

The country of Morocco is part of which continent?

A: Europe

B: Africa

C: Asia

D: North America

13

Which of these has never played James Bond in a film?

A: Pierce Brosnan

B: Harrison Ford

C: Sean Connery

D: Roger Moore

14

What is one most likely to see at the Tate Modern in London?

A: Cars

B: Dinosaurs

C: Paintings

D: Jewels

15

Geometry is studied as a part of which subject?

A: French

B: Mathematics

C: History

D: Geography

50:50 Go to page 250   Go to page 262   ? Answers on page 269

11 ◆ £64,000

16

In which family were Charlotte, Emily and Anne all famous writers?

- A: Brontë
- B: Eliot
- C: Hardy
- D: Austen

17

What name is given to a person on the pitch officiating in a cricket match?

- A: Judge
- B: Referee
- C: Adjudicator
- D: Umpire

18

Which 'cape' is near the southernmost point of Africa?

- A: Well Being
- B: Best Chance
- C: Fine Weather
- D: Good Hope

19

What is the scientific study of animals?

- A: Botany
- B: Zoology
- C: Biology
- D: Geology

20

Which disease, due to a lack of vitamin C, was common on board ships in days gone by?

- A: Scrumpy
- B: Scurvy
- C: Scurry
- D: Scupper

50:50 Go to page 250   Go to page 262   ? Answers on page 269

11 ◆ £64,000

21

In the story by Hans Christian Andersen, what was placed underneath the mattress of the princess?

A: Bean

B: Pea

C: Tomato

D: Carrot

22

Which of the following is not a religion?

A: Shinto

B: Yoga

C: Buddhism

D: Hinduism

23

What is the capital of Egypt?

A: Damascus

B: Athens

C: Amman

D: Cairo

24

Which heavenly body moves around the Earth once every month?

A: Sun

B: Moon

C: Venus

D: North star

25

What is stored at Fort Knox in the USA?

A: Diamonds

B: Oil

C: Silver

D: Gold

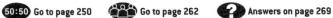 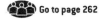

50:50 Go to page 250   Go to page 262   ❓ Answers on page 269

11 ◆ £64,000

26

In which range are the ten highest mountains in the world?

- A: Alps
- B: Rockies
- C: Himalayas
- D: Andes

27

Where did the citrus fruit, the satsuma, originate?

- A: China
- B: Brazil
- C: Japan
- D: Morocco

28

Which product has provided a huge income for many countries in the Middle East?

- A: Coffee
- B: Sugar
- C: Computers
- D: Oil

29

In the story of Peter Pan, what is Wendy's last name?

- A: Dear
- B: Sweet
- C: Darling
- D: Honey

30

Which type of gun has a rotating drum, usually with six chambers?

- A: Rifle
- B: Submachine gun
- C: Machine gun
- D: Revolver

50:50 Go to page 250   Go to page 262   ? Answers on page 269

31

Twickenham is particularly
associated with which sport?

A: Football

B: Rugby

C: Tennis

D: Golf

32

According to the nursery rhyme,
who saw Cock Robin die?

A: Sparrow

B: Fly

C: Fish

D: Beetle

33

In which country did the ancient
Romans found their empire?

A: Italy

B: Norway

C: Great Britain

D: Greece

34

Which of these is a special
pan used in Chinese cookery?

A: Tik

B: Tok

C: Wik

D: Wok

35

How many playing cards are there in a standard pack?

A: 36

B: 40

C: 52

D: 60

50:50 Go to page 250   Go to page 262   ? Answers on page 269

11 ◆ £64,000

36

Which psalm begins with the line
'The Lord is my shepherd'?

A: 1st
B: 23rd
C: 43rd
D: 150th

37

What is the name of the Spice Girls' only movie?

A: Spiceworld the Movie
B: Spicejar the Movie
C: Pickled Spice the Movie
D: Spicebox the Movie

38

Which postal service began in the USA in 1860?

A: Pony Racer
B: Pony Express
C: Pony Dispatch
D: Pony Stage

39

What does the word 'rhinoceros' mean?

A: Big nose
B: Horned nose
C: Thick nose
D: Curved nose

40

Which of these is a deadly spider?

A: Red Death
B: Black Widow
C: Yellow Hell
D: Purple Poison

50:50 Go to page 250 Go to page 262 **?** Answers on page 269

11 ◆ £64,000

41

Calais and Nice are cities in which European country?

A: France
B: Belgium
C: Switzerland
D: The Netherlands

42

Which Disney animated film tells the story of the young King Arthur?

A: The Aristocrats
B: The Black Cauldron
C: The Sword in the Stone
D: The Rescuers

43

How many continents are there in the world?

A: 7
B: 5
C: 9
D: 3

44

Which school boy 'Billy' went to Greyfriars School?

A: Bunter
B: Whizz
C: Smart
D: Elliot

45

Who was The Lone Ranger's special friend and side-kick?

A: Pronto
B: Tonto
C: Tronto
D: Ponto

50:50 Go to page 250   Go to page 262   Answers on page 269

11 ◆ £64,000

46

Which letter has to be placed on the outside of a car to signify the driver has still to pass a test?

A: B

B: X

C: L

D: P

47

Which of these is a famous book by Louisa May Alcott?

A: Little Folks

B: Little Women

C: Little Ladies

D: Little Ones

48

Bob is a shortened form of which name?

A: Robert

B: William

C: Barry

D: Bernard

 50:50 Go to page 250    Go to page 262   ? Answers on page 269

15	£1 MILLION
14	£500,000
13	£250,000
12 ◆	£125,000
11 ◆	£64,000
10 ◆	£32,000
9 ◆	£16,000
8 ◆	£8,000
7 ◆	£4,000
6 ◆	£2,000
5 ◆	£1,000
4 ◆	£500
3 ◆	£300
2 ◆	£200
1 ◆	£100

12 ◆ £125,000

1

In which London street did Sherlock Holmes live?

- A: Harley Street
- B: Regent Street
- C: Baker Street
- D: Oxford Street

2

What covers more than two thirds of the surface of our planet?

- A: Water
- B: Ice
- C: Land
- D: Trees

3

Which actress plays the character Peggy Mitchell in 'EastEnders'?

- A: Wendy Richard
- B: Pam St Clement
- C: Barbara Windsor
- D: Tamzin Outhwaite

4

Who is the Head of State in the United Kingdom?

- A: The Prime Minister
- B: The Queen
- C: The Archbishop of Canterbury
- D: Prince Charles

5

Which 'Benny' was a famous British comedian?

- A: Mound
- B: High
- C: Hill
- D: Bluff

50:50 Go to page 250   Go to page 262   ? Answers on page 269

12 ◆ £125,000

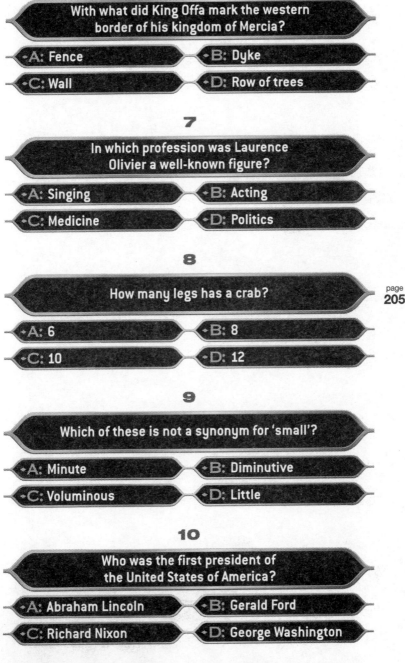

6

With what did King Offa mark the western border of his kingdom of Mercia?

- A: Fence
- B: Dyke
- C: Wall
- D: Row of trees

7

In which profession was Laurence Olivier a well-known figure?

- A: Singing
- B: Acting
- C: Medicine
- D: Politics

8

How many legs has a crab?

- A: 6
- B: 8
- C: 10
- D: 12

9

Which of these is not a synonym for 'small'?

- A: Minute
- B: Diminutive
- C: Voluminous
- D: Little

10

Who was the first president of the United States of America?

- A: Abraham Lincoln
- B: Gerald Ford
- C: Richard Nixon
- D: George Washington

50:50 Go to page 250   Go to page 262   ? Answers on page 269

12 ◆ £125,000

11

Which English architect designed St Paul's Cathedral?

- A: Christopher Robin
- B: Christopher Wren
- C: Christopher Finch
- D: Christopher Bunting

12

By what name was the loud, aggressive rock music of the late 1970s known?

- A: Jazz
- B: Punk
- C: Blues
- D: Reggae

13

In which direction does a magnetic compass needle always point?

- A: North
- B: South
- C: East
- D: West

14

Claustrophobia is a fear of what?

- A: Spiders
- B: Heights
- C: Water
- D: Confined spaces

15

In 2001, Sir Alex Ferguson was the manager of which football club?

- A: Everton
- B: Liverpool
- C: Manchester United
- D: Aston Villa

50:50 Go to page 251   Go to page 263   Answers on page 269

12 ◆ £125,000

16

In 'Alice Through the Looking Glass', what did Tweedledum and Tweedledee agree to do?

- A: Have breakfast
- B: Have a battle
- C: Have a party
- D: Have a bath

17

For what is Benjamin Britten famous?

- A: Poetry
- B: Plays
- C: Novels
- D: Music

18

Which of these is a famous sculpture by Michelangelo?

- A: David
- B: Mark
- C: Thomas
- D: Peter

19

What sort of 'jelly' do bees make?

- A: Royal
- B: Lemon
- C: Champagne
- D: Mint

20

Which of the following is not a vitamin?

- A: A
- B: B
- C: C
- D: X

50:50 Go to page 251   Go to page 263   Answers on page 269

21

What is the name for baby squirrels?

A: Nutkins
B: Kittens
C: Squirrelets
D: Mittens

22

Prior to Elizabeth II, who was the last reigning British queen?

A: Victoria
B: Elizabeth I
C: Anne
D: Mary II

23

Which saint is particularly associated with the Italian town of Assisi?

A: St Francis
B: St Nicholas
C: St Patrick
D: St George

24

What was the first name of Einstein, the famous 20th century scientist?

A: Arnold
B: Albert
C: Arthur
D: Alfred

25

To which 'Star Trek' character is the catchphrase 'Beam me up Scotty' attributed?

A: Captain Kirk
B: Spock
C: Dr McCoy
D: Sulu

50:50 Go to page 251　　Go to page 263　　Answers on page 269

12 ◆ £125,000

26

At what age can you legally buy a pet in the UK?

- A: 8
- B: 10
- C: 12
- D: 14

27

Which of these books was written by Rudyard Kipling?

- A: The Forest Letters
- B: The Jungle Book
- C: The Swamp Series
- D: The Tree Trilogy

28

What name is given to a number multiplied by itself?

- A: Root
- B: Square
- C: Binary
- D: Googol

29

Which of these is a large powerful computer?

- A: Bigblock
- B: Greatform
- C: Mainframe
- D: Grandplan

30

What 'colour' is the political party whose aims are based on concern for the environment?

- A: Red
- B: Blue
- C: Green
- D: Yellow

50:50 Go to page 251   Go to page 263   ? Answers on page 269

12 ◆ £125,000

31

Paddington, King's Cross and Waterloo
are all railway stations in which city?

A: Manchester
B: London
C: Edinburgh
D: Bristol

32

Which film of 2001 starred
Nicole Kidman and Ewan McGregor?

A: Eiffel Tower
B: Notre Dame
C: Arc de Triomphe
D: Moulin Rouge

33

What name is given to the process of breathing
in air and breathing out carbon dioxide?

A: Saturation
B: Condensation
C: Evaporation
D: Respiration

34

In 1994, Nelson Mandela became
which country's first black president?

A: New Zealand
B: Australia
C: South Africa
D: USA

35

What did England host for the first time in 1966?

A: Olympic Games
B: Eurovision Song Contest
C: Football World Cup
D: Miss World Contest

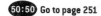 50:50 Go to page 251    Go to page 263    Answers on page 269

36

How many sides has a hexagon?

A: 4

B: 6

C: 8

D: 10

37

Which one of the twelve apostles was 'doubting'?

A: Matthew

B: Mark

C: Thomas

D: Peter

38

What are the leather covers worn by cowboys to protect their trousers called?

A: Ponchos

B: Chaps

C: Guys

D: Wranglers

39

Which of these is another word for the grasslands of North America?

A: Range

B: Steppes

C: Wilderness

D: Tundra

40

What is the measure of the amount of space that an object takes up?

A: Area

B: Volume

C: Weight

D: Depth

12 ◆ £125,000

41

The Financial Times is printed on which colour paper?

A: White

B: Blue

C: Pink

D: Yellow

42

Who wrote 'Double Act' and 'The Bed and Breakfast Star'?

A: Enid Blyton

B: J K Rowling

C: Jacqueline Wilson

D: Roald Dahl

43

Which part of speech describes a noun?

A: Verb

B: Adverb

C: Adjective

D: Pronoun

44

In ancient Rome, what was the job of a galley slave?

A: Cleaning the kitchen

B: Polishing the silver

C: Rowing the boat

D: Unloading the ship

50:50 Go to page 251   Go to page 263   ? Answers on page 269

15	£1 MILLION
14	£500,000
13 ◆	**£250,000**
12 ◆	£125,000
11 ◆	£64,000
10 ◆	**£32,000**
9 ◆	£16,000
8 ◆	£8,000
7 ◆	£4,000
6 ◆	£2,000
5 ◆	**£1,000**
4 ◆	£500
3 ◆	£300
2 ◆	£200
1 ◆	£100

13 ◆ £250,000

1

From which country did the seventies group Abba originate?

◆A: USA   ◆B: Sweden

◆C: Germany   ◆D: Denmark

2

What is the Matterhorn?

◆A: Musical instrument   ◆B: Car alarm

◆C: Mountain   ◆D: Ice cream

3

Which type of angle measures less than 90 degrees?

◆A: Right   ◆B: Obtuse

◆C: Acute   ◆D: Reflex

4

What number is represented by the Roman numeral L?

◆A: 5   ◆B: 10

◆C: 50   ◆D: 100

5

In which year did the Great Fire of London take place?

◆A: 1466   ◆B: 1666

◆C: 1866   ◆D: 1966

 50:50 Go to page 251    Go to page 263   ? Answers on page 269

13 ◆ £250,000

6

What is a 'penny black'?

A: Postage stamp
B: Liquorice sweet
C: Old coin
D: Shoe polish

7

Which is Britain's largest theme park?

A: Legoland
B: Alton Towers
C: Thorpe Park
D: Blackpool Pleasure Beach

8

Who wrote the books 'Great Expectations' and 'Oliver Twist'?

A: William Shakespeare
B: Thomas Hardy
C: Charles Dickens
D: D H Lawrence

9

Which is the largest continent in the world?

A: Europe
B: Africa
C: Asia
D: Antarctica

10

Paediatrics is the medical study of what?

A: Feet
B: Children
C: Gums
D: Hair

50:50 Go to page 251   Go to page 263   ? Answers on page 269

13 ◆ £250,000

11

Which of the following is a famous fable by Aesop?

A: The Hare and the Tortoise

B: The Rabbit and the Snake

C: The Mouse and the Snail

D: The Rat and the Cat

12

Who was appointed UK Foreign Secretary in June 2001?

A: Jack Hay

B: Jack Straw

C: Jack Bedding

D: Jack Corn

13

In which blockbuster film of 2001 did Daniel Radcliffe play the leading role?

A: Harry Potter and the Philosopher's Stone

B: Stuart Little

C: Jurassic Park III

D: Cats and Dogs

14

How many oceans are there on Earth?

A: 10

B: 7

C: 5

D: 4

15

Which words did Dorothy recite in the 'Wizard of Oz' to transport her back to Kansas?

A: 'There's no place like home'

B: 'Home is where the heart is'

C: 'Home on the range'

D: 'The Great Oz has spoken'

50:50 Go to page 251   Go to page 263   Answers on page 269

13 ◆ £250,000

16

What does 'geo' mean, as in geography?

A: Map
B: Ocean
C: Earth
D: Space

17

Nefertiti was queen of which country?

A: India
B: Greece
C: Egypt
D: China

18

In which English county is the port of Dover?

A: Kent
B: Devon
C: Essex
D: Suffolk

19

What is the fourth dimension?

A: Length
B: Breadth
C: Height
D: Time

20

In which year was Elizabeth II crowned?

A: 1923
B: 1933
C: 1953
D: 1983

50:50 Go to page 251   Go to page 263   ? Answers on page 269

13 ◆ £250,000

21

How is Queen Cleopatra of Egypt said to have died?

A: Attacked by a tiger
B: Fell from a horse
C: Snake bite
D: Scorpion sting

22

In music, which sign cancels a sharp or flat?

A: Normal
B: Natural
C: Simple
D: Open

23

What does the word 'video' mean in the original Latin?

A: I hear
B: I speak
C: I see
D: I smell

24

Which planet is famous for its 'rings'?

A: Mars
B: Saturn
C: Pluto
D: Venus

25

How many edges has a fifty pence piece?

A: 5
B: 7
C: 9
D: 10

50:50 Go to page 251   Go to page 263   ? Answers on page 269

26

Which of these dinosaurs could fly?

A: Triceratops
B: Stegosaurus
C: Tyrannosaurus
D: Pterodactyl

27

Who became the Princess Royal in 1987?

A: Princess Anne
B: Princess Margaret
C: Princess Alexandra
D: Princess Eugenie

28

Which gas constitutes approximately 20% of the air we breathe?

A: Oxygen
B: Nitrogen
C: Hydrogen
D: Carbon dioxide

29

How many states make up the United States of America?

A: 25
B: 50
C: 75
D: 100

30

Which of these titles is given to the eldest son of the British sovereign?

A: Prince of England
B: Prince of Wales
C: Prince of Scotland
D: Prince of Ireland

 50:50 Go to page 251   Go to page 263   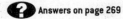 ? Answers on page 269

31

What is the name of the hot, spicy sausage often used as a pizza topping?

A: Pepperoni
B: Paprika
C: Pepper
D: Peroni

32

Which of these are stories by Rudyard Kipling?

A: Just So
B: The Very Thing
C: The Honest Truth
D: By All Means

33

What name is given to fish such as halibut, plaice and sole?

A: Levelfish
B: Boardfish
C: Flatfish
D: Platefish

34

Which London borough includes Buckingham Palace and the Houses of Parliament?

A: Westminster
B: St James
C: Soho
D: Mayfair

35

What is the chemical symbol for iron?

A: Fe
B: H
C: O
D: Po

50:50 Go to page 251   Go to page 263   ? Answers on page 269

13 ◆ £250,000

36

Which 'William' in Swiss legend shot an apple from his son's head with a crossbow?

- A: William the Conqueror
- B: William Tell
- C: William of Orange
- D: Prince William

37

When driving a car, what speed must you not exceed on a motorway in the UK?

- A: 40 mph
- B: 50 mph
- C: 60 mph
- D: 70 mph

page **221**

38

With which sport is the Czech-born star Martina Navratilova associated?

- A: Tennis
- B: Golf
- C: Skiing
- D: Badminton

39

Who was the Roman god of love?

- A: Neptune
- B: Apollo
- C: Cupid
- D: Mars

40

Which of the following is not a fielding position in cricket?

- A: Silly point
- B: Third man
- C: Fine leg
- D: Complete cover

 50:50 Go to page 251   Go to page 263   ? Answers on page 269

15	£1 MILLION
14 ◆	£500,000
13 ◆	£250,000
12 ◆	£125,000
11 ◆	£64,000
10 ◆	£32,000
9 ◆	£16,000
8 ◆	£8,000
7 ◆	£4,000
6 ◆	£2,000
5 ◆	£1,000
4 ◆	£500
3 ◆	£300
2 ◆	£200
1 ◆	£100

14 ◆ £500,000

1

What live in a formicary?

A: Bees

B: Ants

C: Wasps

D: Eels

2

Which toy shop in London is said to be the 'largest in the world'?

A: Hamsons

B: Hamptons

C: Hamleys

D: Hammonds

3

What name is given to the inland region of Australia?

A: Infront

B: Sidelines

C: Outback

D: Downunder

4

Which member of the Royal family began a course at St Andrews University in 2001?

A: Prince Harry

B: Peter Phillips

C: Prince William

D: Zara Phillips

5

In the periodic table, what is the atomic number for Hydrogen?

A: 20

B: 1

C: 30

D: 2

50:50 Go to page 252   Go to page 264   ❓ Answers on page 270

14 ◆ £500,000

6

Which monarch ruled Great Britain for 63 years, longer than any other?

A: Henry VIII
B: Victoria
C: Elizabeth I
D: William the Conqueror

7

The five Great Lakes lie on the border between which two countries?

A: Canada and USA
B: USA and Mexico
C: China and India
D: Brazil and Peru

8

What name was given to the emblem or flag carried into battle by every Roman legion?

A: Standard
B: Ensign
C: Banner
D: Tricolour

9

In days gone by, which plant was used to crown the Olympic winners?

A: Laurel
B: Holly
C: Willow
D: Mistletoe

10

What is the name of the family in the 'Little House on the Prairie' stories?

A: Wingalls
B: Pringles
C: Ingalls
D: Tingalls

50:50 Go to page 252   Go to page 264   ❓ Answers on page 270

14 ◆ £500,000

11

In which US city was President John
F Kennedy assassinated in 1963?

- A: Washington
- B: Los Angeles
- C: Chicago
- D: Dallas

12

Where does a peanut grow?

- A: Underground
- B: On the branch of a tree
- C: On a sand dune
- D: In the sea

13

In which profession was Christiaan Barnard a pioneer?

- A: Teaching
- B: Medicine
- C: Architecture
- D: Law

14

For what was Charles Blondin particularly famous?

- A: Fire eating
- B: Lion taming
- C: Tightrope-walking
- D: Clowning

15

Which of these is a shopping complex in Birmingham?

- A: The Bull Ring
- B: The Brum Ring
- C: The Horse Ring
- D: The Circus Ring

50:50 Go to page 252   Go to page 264   **?** Answers on page 270

14 ◆ £500,000

16

In geometry, what is a three dimensional shape?

- A: Solid
- B: Plane
- C: Angle
- D: Coordinate

17

Which English scientist is best known for his 'Theory of Evolution'?

- A: Watt
- B: Newton
- C: Darwin
- D: Rutherford

18

What was the name of the Ancient Egyptian system of picture writing?

- A: Graffiti
- B: Cave painting
- C: Hieroglyphics
- D: Engraving

19

Which American magician shares his name with the title of a book by Charles Dickens?

- A: David Copperfield
- B: Nicholas Nickleby
- C: Oliver Twist
- D: Edwin Drood

20

What is the average, normal temperature of the human body in degrees Celsius?

- A: 33 C
- B: 35 C
- C: 37 C
- D: 39 C

50:50 Go to page 252　　Go to page 264　　**?** Answers on page 270

14 ◆ £500,000

21

In the Christian calendar, which day marks Christ's triumphal entry into Jerusalem?

- A: Christmas Day
- B: Ash Wednesday
- C: Palm Sunday
- D: Shrove Tuesday

22

In weather terms, what is a mixture of rain and snow?

- A: Frost
- B: Dew
- C: Sleet
- D: Mist

23

'The Canterbury Tales' was written by which great English writer?

- A: Chaucer
- B: Shakespeare
- C: Dickens
- D: Stevenson

24

How many notes are there in an octave?

- A: 4
- B: 6
- C: 8
- D: 10

25

In terms of area, which is the largest country in the world?

- A: Russia
- B: Brazil
- C: Canada
- D: USA

14 ◆ £500,000

26

What word describes animals that eat only plants?

- A: Herbivores
- B: Carnivores
- C: Omnivores
- D: Insectivores

27

Which well known TV personality presents 'Children in Need' for the BBC?

- A: Terry Wogan
- B: Cilla Black
- C: Des O'Connor
- D: Dale Winton

28

What are cows said to chew when they regurgitate their food?

page **229**

- A: The chaff
- B: The cud
- C: The turf
- D: The bud

29

Which marine creatures often attach themselves to the bottom of boats?

- A: Lobsters
- B: Cockles
- C: Barnacles
- D: Whelks

30

In football, what is taken when the defending team puts the ball out of play behind their own goal-line?

- A: Corner kick
- B: Free kick
- C: Penalty
- D: Throw in

50:50 Go to page 252   Go to page 264   ? Answers on page 270

14 ◆ £500,000

31

Which is the only rock that can float?

A: Pumice

B: Granite

C: Marble

D: Slate

32

In athletics, what would you do with the 'shot'?

A: Throw it

B: Put it

C: Place it

D: Hurl it

33

Which gas is used in glass tubes to make coloured light sources and signs?

A: Helium

B: Oxygen

C: Hydrogen

D: Neon

34

In a 1997 film, Will Smith and Tommy Lee Jones were 'Men in...' what?

A: Black

B: Blue

C: Red

D: Green

35

During 2001, which fast-food company sponsored 'The Simpsons' TV programme on Sky One?

A: Pizza Express

B: Kentucky Fried Chicken

C: Pizza Hut

D: Domino Pizza

50:50 Go to page 252   Go to page 264   **?** Answers on page 270

14 ◆ £500,000

36

Jenny, Liz and Tash are members of which girl band?

- A: Destiny's Child
- B: Steps
- C: B*Witched
- D: Atomic Kitten

15	◆	**£1 MILLION**
14	◆	£500,000
13	◆	£250,000
12	◆	£125,000
11	◆	£64,000
10	◆	£32,000
9	◆	£16,000
8	◆	£8,000
7	◆	£4,000
6	◆	£2,000
5	◆	£1,000
4	◆	£500
3	◆	£300
2	◆	£200
1	◆	£100

15 ◆ £1,000,000

1

In which decade was the Great Depression?

A: 1920s

B: 1930s

C: 1940s

D: 1950s

2

Which of these was written by the
Russian composer Igor Stravinsky?

A: The Firebird

B: The Bluebird

C: The Robin

D: The Magpie

3

Who is not a member of Just
William's gang, the Outlaws?

A: Henry

B: Douglas

C: Ginger

D: Robert

4

Which motorway runs between London and Bristol?

A: M1

B: M3

C: M4

D: M6

5

What name is given to the main body of a snail?

A: Hand

B: Arm

C: Leg

D: Foot

50:50 Go to page 252   Go to page 264   Answers on page 270

15 ◆ £1,000,000

6

Which UK high street bank has
a black horse as its symbol?

A: Lloyds TSB
B: Barclays
C: HSBC
D: Royal Bank of Scotland

7

Which animal is sacred to Hindus?

A: Sheep
B: Chicken
C: Cow
D: Cat

8

On average, how many times does a human
heart beat per minute when resting?

A: 20 - 30
B: 60 - 70
C: 100 - 110
D: 130 - 140

9

Which of these is an old-fashioned style of trouser?

A: Plus threes
B: Plus fours
C: Plus fives
D: Plus sixes

10

What name is given to a one-humped camel?

A: Bactrian
B: Balkan
C: Cassowary
D: Dromedary

 50:50 Go to page 252   Go to page 264   ❓ Answers on page 270

15 ◆ £1,000,000

11

Which of these words is not onomatopoeic?

A: Sizzle
B: Squelch
C: Hiss
D: Fry

12

The statue of the Little Mermaid is in which European city?

A: Paris
B: Rome
C: Copenhagen
D: Madrid

13

Which river insect uses its paddle-like legs to row across the surface of the water?

A: Water boatman
B: River glider
C: The fisherman
D: Flying ship

14

What is the name of former US president Bill Clinton's wife?

A: Barbara
B: Susan
C: Helen
D: Hillary

15

Which of these British universities is the oldest?

A: Cambridge
B: Exeter
C: Reading
D: Birmingham

50:50 Go to page 252   Go to page 264   ? Answers on page 270

15 ◆ £1,000,000

16

In Scrabble, what is the value of the letter Z?

A: 6   B: 8

C: 10   D: 12

17

Which is the only man-made structure once said to be visible from the moon?

A: Pyramids   B: Great Wall of China

C: Buckingham Palace   D: Sydney Opera House

18

New York City stands on which river?

A: Hudson   B: Nile

C: Mississippi   D: Seine

19

Which liquid metal is used in thermometers?

A: Copper   B: Mercury

C: Silver   D: Nickel

20

How many years as monarch did Queen Elizabeth II celebrate at her silver jubilee?

A: 10   B: 20

C: 25   D: 50

50:50 Go to page 252   Go to page 264   ? Answers on page 270

21

Which of these is a famous painting by Vincent Van Gogh?

- A: Bluebells
- B: Snowdrops
- C: Sunflowers
- D: Marigolds

22

What name is given to a group of kangaroos?

- A: Horde
- B: Army
- C: Mob
- D: Crowd

23

Which bus company in the USA is named after a breed of dog?

- A: Greyhound
- B: Labrador
- C: Bloodhound
- D: Poodle

24

In the USA, what name is given to a postcode?

- A: Zone code
- B: Belt code
- C: Zip code
- D: Block code

25

Which blockbuster film of 1996 was the first to be entirely computer generated?

- A: James and the Giant Peach
- B: Pocahontas
- C: Toy Story
- D: Hercules

50:50 Go to page 252   Go to page 264   ? Answers on page 270

15 ◆ £1,000,000

26

In which modern day country was the ancient civilization of the Incas centred?

A: Brazil
B: Mexico
C: India
D: Peru

27

What height is a tennis net at the centre?

A: 2 feet / 60.9cm
B: 3 feet / 91.4cm
C: 4 feet / 1.22m
D: 5 feet / 1.52m

28

Which of these means an arrangement of musical notes on paper?

A: Mark
B: Count
C: Stroke
D: Score

29

What is the approximate population of the world?

A: Six billion
B: Six hundred million
C: Six million
D: Six hundred thousand

30

Which scale is used to measure earthquakes?

A: Richter
B: Celsius
C: Beaufort
D: Fahrenheit

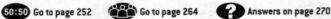 50:50 Go to page 252   Go to page 264   ? Answers on page 270

15 ◆ £1,000,000

31

How many coloured balls are used in a game of snooker?

A: 11

B: 17

C: 22

D: 30

32

Which family acquired Mary Poppins as a nursemaid?

A: The Butchers

B: The Banks

C: The Bakers

D: The Brewers

50:50 Go to page 252   Go to page 264   Answers on page 270

50:50

£100

1	Options remaining are C and D	38	Options remaining are A and D
2	Options remaining are A and D	39	Options remaining are A and D
3	Options remaining are A and D	40	Options remaining are A and D
4	Options remaining are A and C	41	Options remaining are A and D
5	Options remaining are B and C	42	Options remaining are C and D
6	Options remaining are A and B	43	Options remaining are B and C
7	Options remaining are A and C	44	Options remaining are B and C
8	Options remaining are B and C	45	Options remaining are A and C
9	Options remaining are B and C	46	Options remaining are A and D
10	Options remaining are A and B	47	Options remaining are B and D
11	Options remaining are A and C	48	Options remaining are C and D
12	Options remaining are B and C	49	Options remaining are A and B
13	Options remaining are A and D	50	Options remaining are A and C
14	Options remaining are A and B	51	Options remaining are B and D
15	Options remaining are A and C	52	Options remaining are A and C
16	Options remaining are B and C	53	Options remaining are A and D
17	Options remaining are A and C	54	Options remaining are A and B
18	Options remaining are A and D	55	Options remaining are B and D
19	Options remaining are C and D	56	Options remaining are C and D
20	Options remaining are A and B	57	Options remaining are B and C
21	Options remaining are B and C	58	Options remaining are A and B
22	Options remaining are C and D	59	Options remaining are A and D
23	Options remaining are B and D	60	Options remaining are B and C
24	Options remaining are B and C	61	Options remaining are A and B
25	Options remaining are C and D	62	Options remaining are A and C
26	Options remaining are B and C	63	Options remaining are A and D
27	Options remaining are A and B	64	Options remaining are C and D
28	Options remaining are A and B	65	Options remaining are A and D
29	Options remaining are A and D	66	Options remaining are C and D
30	Options remaining are A and C	67	Options remaining are B and C
31	Options remaining are B and C	68	Options remaining are C and D
32	Options remaining are C and D	69	Options remaining are A and B
33	Options remaining are B and C	70	Options remaining are B and C
34	Options remaining are A and B	71	Options remaining are A and C
35	Options remaining are A and C	72	Options remaining are C and D
36	Options remaining are C and D	73	Options remaining are B and C
37	Options remaining are B and C	74	Options remaining are B and C

50:50

£200

50:50

65	Options remaining are A and B	75	Options remaining are B and D
66	Options remaining are C and D	76	Options remaining are A and C
67	Options remaining are A and C	77	Options remaining are B and D
68	Options remaining are A and D	78	Options remaining are C and D
69	Options remaining are B and C	79	Options remaining are A and D
70	Options remaining are A and B	80	Options remaining are B and C
71	Options remaining are A and B	81	Options remaining are A and B
72	Options remaining are B and D	82	Options remaining are A and D
73	Options remaining are A and D	83	Options remaining are A and B
74	Options remaining are A and D	84	Options remaining are A and B

£300

1	Options remaining are A and B	30	Options remaining are B and D
2	Options remaining are A and D	31	Options remaining are A and B
3	Options remaining are C and D	32	Options remaining are A and B
4	Options remaining are B and D	33	Options remaining are A and C
5	Options remaining are A and D	34	Options remaining are A and B
6	Options remaining are A and B	35	Options remaining are C and D
7	Options remaining are A and B	36	Options remaining are A and C
8	Options remaining are B and D	37	Options remaining are A and B
9	Options remaining are C and D	38	Options remaining are A and D
10	Options remaining are B and D	39	Options remaining are B and C
11	Options remaining are A and B	40	Options remaining are A and C
12	Options remaining are C and D	41	Options remaining are A and D
13	Options remaining are A and B	42	Options remaining are B and C
14	Options remaining are B and D	43	Options remaining are B and D
15	Options remaining are A and C	44	Options remaining are A and D
16	Options remaining are B and D	45	Options remaining are B and D
17	Options remaining are A and B	46	Options remaining are A and B
18	Options remaining are A and B	47	Options remaining are A and C
19	Options remaining are B and D	48	Options remaining are C and D
20	Options remaining are B and C	49	Options remaining are B and C
21	Options remaining are B and D	50	Options remaining are C and D
22	Options remaining are A and C	51	Options remaining are A and D
23	Options remaining are C and D	52	Options remaining are B and C
24	Options remaining are A and C	53	Options remaining are A and D
25	Options remaining are B and C	54	Options remaining are A and B
26	Options remaining are C and D	55	Options remaining are A and C
27	Options remaining are B and C	56	Options remaining are B and C
28	Options remaining are B and C	57	Options remaining are A and D
29	Options remaining are A and B	58	Options remaining are A and B

50:50

59	Options remaining are C and D	70	Options remaining are B and D
60	Options remaining are B and D	71	Options remaining are B and C
61	Options remaining are B and C	72	Options remaining are A and C
62	Options remaining are B and D	73	Options remaining are B and C
63	Options remaining are A and B	74	Options remaining are B and C
64	Options remaining are A and D	75	Options remaining are A and C
65	Options remaining are A and D	76	Options remaining are C and D
66	Options remaining are B and C	77	Options remaining are A and B
67	Options remaining are B and D	78	Options remaining are B and D
68	Options remaining are A and C	79	Options remaining are B and C
69	Options remaining are A and C	80	Options remaining are A and B

£500

1	Options remaining are A and B	29	Options remaining are A and B
2	Options remaining are A and C	30	Options remaining are B and C
3	Options remaining are A and D	31	Options remaining are A and B
4	Options remaining are B and D	32	Options remaining are C and D
5	Options remaining are A and D	33	Options remaining are A and D
6	Options remaining are C and D	34	Options remaining are B and C
7	Options remaining are A and D	35	Options remaining are A and B
8	Options remaining are C and D	36	Options remaining are A and D
9	Options remaining are B and C	37	Options remaining are A and B
10	Options remaining are A and D	38	Options remaining are A and C
11	Options remaining are B and D	39	Options remaining are B and C
12	Options remaining are A and B	40	Options remaining are A and B
13	Options remaining are B and C	41	Options remaining are B and D
14	Options remaining are B and C	42	Options remaining are A and D
15	Options remaining are A and C	43	Options remaining are B and C
16	Options remaining are C and D	44	Options remaining are A and C
17	Options remaining are A and D	45	Options remaining are A and C
18	Options remaining are B and C	46	Options remaining are B and D
19	Options remaining are B and C	47	Options remaining are B and D
20	Options remaining are A and B	48	Options remaining are A and D
21	Options remaining are A and D	49	Options remaining are C and D
22	Options remaining are C and D	50	Options remaining are B and C
23	Options remaining are A and C	51	Options remaining are B and D
24	Options remaining are A and B	52	Options remaining are A and D
25	Options remaining are B and C	53	Options remaining are B and D
26	Options remaining are A and D	54	Options remaining are A and B
27	Options remaining are B and C	55	Options remaining are B and D
28	Options remaining are B and C	56	Options remaining are A and C

50:50

57	Options remaining are B and C	67	Options remaining are B and D
58	Options remaining are A and B	68	Options remaining are A and D
59	Options remaining are C and D	69	Options remaining are A and B
60	Options remaining are C and D	70	Options remaining are B and C
61	Options remaining are C and D	71	Options remaining are A and B
62	Options remaining are B and C	72	Options remaining are A and C
63	Options remaining are B and D	73	Options remaining are B and D
64	Options remaining are B and D	74	Options remaining are A and C
65	Options remaining are A and B	75	Options remaining are C and D
66	Options remaining are A and B	76	Options remaining are B and D

£1,000

1	Options remaining are A and D	30	Options remaining are B and D
2	Options remaining are B and D	31	Options remaining are C and D
3	Options remaining are C and D	32	Options remaining are A and D
4	Options remaining are A and D	33	Options remaining are B and C
5	Options remaining are A and B	34	Options remaining are C and D
6	Options remaining are C and D	35	Options remaining are C and D
7	Options remaining are B and C	36	Options remaining are B and D
8	Options remaining are B and C	37	Options remaining are C and D
9	Options remaining are A and C	38	Options remaining are A and C
10	Options remaining are B and C	39	Options remaining are B and C
11	Options remaining are B and D	40	Options remaining are A and C
12	Options remaining are B and D	41	Options remaining are B and D
13	Options remaining are B and D	42	Options remaining are B and C
14	Options remaining are A and B	43	Options remaining are A and C
15	Options remaining are B and D	44	Options remaining are A and C
16	Options remaining are A and B	45	Options remaining are B and D
17	Options remaining are A and B	46	Options remaining are C and D
18	Options remaining are B and D	47	Options remaining are C and D
19	Options remaining are B and C	48	Options remaining are B and C
20	Options remaining are C and D	49	Options remaining are A and B
21	Options remaining are B and D	50	Options remaining are C and D
22	Options remaining are B and D	51	Options remaining are C and D
23	Options remaining are A and D	52	Options remaining are B and D
24	Options remaining are A and B	53	Options remaining are A and D
25	Options remaining are B and C	54	Options remaining are B and C
26	Options remaining are A and B	55	Options remaining are C and D
27	Options remaining are B and D	56	Options remaining are B and C
28	Options remaining are B and D	57	Options remaining are B and D
29	Options remaining are B and D	58	Options remaining are C and D

50:50

59	Options remaining are C and D	66	Options remaining are B and C
60	Options remaining are A and D	67	Options remaining are B and C
61	Options remaining are A and D	68	Options remaining are C and D
62	Options remaining are C and D	69	Options remaining are A and D
63	Options remaining are B and D	70	Options remaining are A and B
64	Options remaining are A and B	71	Options remaining are C and D
65	Options remaining are A and C	72	Options remaining are B and C

£2,000

1	Options remaining are B and D	32	Options remaining are A and C
2	Options remaining are A and D	33	Options remaining are A and B
3	Options remaining are B and D	34	Options remaining are A and B
4	Options remaining are A and B	35	Options remaining are B and C
5	Options remaining are B and C	36	Options remaining are C and D
6	Options remaining are A and B	37	Options remaining are C and D
7	Options remaining are A and B	38	Options remaining are A and B
8	Options remaining are A and C	39	Options remaining are A and B
9	Options remaining are A and C	40	Options remaining are C and D
10	Options remaining are A and D	41	Options remaining are B and D
11	Options remaining are A and B	42	Options remaining are A and B
12	Options remaining are A and D	43	Options remaining are A and B
13	Options remaining are A and B	44	Options remaining are C and D
14	Options remaining are B and C	45	Options remaining are C and D
15	Options remaining are B and D	46	Options remaining are A and B
16	Options remaining are B and D	47	Options remaining are B and C
17	Options remaining are B and D	48	Options remaining are A and B
18	Options remaining are B and D	49	Options remaining are A and B
19	Options remaining are A and C	50	Options remaining are A and C
20	Options remaining are A and D	51	Options remaining are C and D
21	Options remaining are B and D	52	Options remaining are B and C
22	Options remaining are A and D	53	Options remaining are A and B
23	Options remaining are B and C	54	Options remaining are B and C
24	Options remaining are A and B	55	Options remaining are B and C
25	Options remaining are C and D	56	Options remaining are B and C
26	Options remaining are A and C	57	Options remaining are C and D
27	Options remaining are A and D	58	Options remaining are A and B
28	Options remaining are A and C	59	Options remaining are B and C
29	Options remaining are B and C	60	Options remaining are B and C
30	Options remaining are C and D	61	Options remaining are B and C
31	Options remaining are A and B	62	Options remaining are B and C

50:50

63 Options remaining are A and D
64 Options remaining are C and D
65 Options remaining are C and D

66 Options remaining are B and C
67 Options remaining are B and C
68 Options remaining are B and D

£4,000

1   Options remaining are B and D
2   Options remaining are A and B
3   Options remaining are A and D
4   Options remaining are A and C
5   Options remaining are C and D
6   Options remaining are A and C
7   Options remaining are A and D
8   Options remaining are B and C
9   Options remaining are A and B
10 Options remaining are A and B
11 Options remaining are B and D
12 Options remaining are B and D
13 Options remaining are B and C
14 Options remaining are A and D
15 Options remaining are A and C
16 Options remaining are A and D
17 Options remaining are A and B
18 Options remaining are A and D
19 Options remaining are A and B
20 Options remaining are A and D
21 Options remaining are C and D
22 Options remaining are A and C
23 Options remaining are A and B
24 Options remaining are B and C
25 Options remaining are A and B
26 Options remaining are A and C
27 Options remaining are C and D
28 Options remaining are A and C
29 Options remaining are C and D
30 Options remaining are B and C
31 Options remaining are B and D
32 Options remaining are A and B

33 Options remaining are A and D
34 Options remaining are A and C
35 Options remaining are A and C
36 Options remaining are B and C
37 Options remaining are B and D
38 Options remaining are A and D
39 Options remaining are A and B
40 Options remaining are B and D
41 Options remaining are A and C
42 Options remaining are A and B
43 Options remaining are B and C
44 Options remaining are B and C
45 Options remaining are B and D
46 Options remaining are A and D
47 Options remaining are A and D
48 Options remaining are A and D
49 Options remaining are B and C
50 Options remaining are B and C
51 Options remaining are A and B
52 Options remaining are B and C
53 Options remaining are A and C
54 Options remaining are A and B
55 Options remaining are A and B
56 Options remaining are B and C
57 Options remaining are A and B
58 Options remaining are C and D
59 Options remaining are B and C
60 Options remaining are A and C
61 Options remaining are B and C
62 Options remaining are A and D
63 Options remaining are A and B
64 Options remaining are C and D

50:50

£8,000

1	Options remaining are C and D	31	Options remaining are C and D
2	Options remaining are A and B	32	Options remaining are A and B
3	Options remaining are A and B	33	Options remaining are A and C
4	Options remaining are A and B	34	Options remaining are B and D
5	Options remaining are A and D	35	Options remaining are B and D
6	Options remaining are B and D	36	Options remaining are A and C
7	Options remaining are A and D	37	Options remaining are A and C
8	Options remaining are C and D	38	Options remaining are A and B
9	Options remaining are C and D	39	Options remaining are B and C
10	Options remaining are B and D	40	Options remaining are A and B
11	Options remaining are A and D	41	Options remaining are C and D
12	Options remaining are A and C	42	Options remaining are C and D
13	Options remaining are A and C	43	Options remaining are C and D
14	Options remaining are A and B	44	Options remaining are A and B
15	Options remaining are A and B	45	Options remaining are B and D
16	Options remaining are B and C	46	Options remaining are B and D
17	Options remaining are A and D	47	Options remaining are B and C
18	Options remaining are B and C	48	Options remaining are B and C
19	Options remaining are B and C	49	Options remaining are A and C
20	Options remaining are B and D	50	Options remaining are A and D
21	Options remaining are B and C	51	Options remaining are A and C
22	Options remaining are C and D	52	Options remaining are A and B
23	Options remaining are C and D	53	Options remaining are A and B
24	Options remaining are C and D	54	Options remaining are B and C
25	Options remaining are B and C	55	Options remaining are A and C
26	Options remaining are A and C	56	Options remaining are A and B
27	Options remaining are B and D	57	Options remaining are B and C
28	Options remaining are B and D	58	Options remaining are B and C
29	Options remaining are B and D	59	Options remaining are C and D
30	Options remaining are A and B	60	Options remaining are A and B

£16,000

1	Options remaining are B and C	10	Options remaining are C and D
2	Options remaining are A and C	11	Options remaining are A and B
3	Options remaining are B and D	12	Options remaining are C and D
4	Options remaining are A and D	13	Options remaining are A and C
5	Options remaining are B and C	14	Options remaining are A and B
6	Options remaining are A and C	15	Options remaining are B and C
7	Options remaining are C and D	16	Options remaining are B and C
8	Options remaining are C and D	17	Options remaining are B and D
9	Options remaining are A and C	18	Options remaining are A and D

50:50

19	Options remaining are A and C	38	Options remaining are C and D
20	Options remaining are A and B	39	Options remaining are A and C
21	Options remaining are A and B	40	Options remaining are B and C
22	Options remaining are B and C	41	Options remaining are A and C
23	Options remaining are A and C	42	Options remaining are B and C
24	Options remaining are B and C	43	Options remaining are C and D
25	Options remaining are A and B	44	Options remaining are B and C
26	Options remaining are A and C	45	Options remaining are A and B
27	Options remaining are A and B	46	Options remaining are A and D
28	Options remaining are B and C	47	Options remaining are A and B
29	Options remaining are C and D	48	Options remaining are A and B
30	Options remaining are B and D	49	Options remaining are A and B
31	Options remaining are C and D	50	Options remaining are A and B
32	Options remaining are A and C	51	Options remaining are A and D
33	Options remaining are C and D	52	Options remaining are A and C
34	Options remaining are C and D	53	Options remaining are A and B
35	Options remaining are B and D	54	Options remaining are C and D
36	Options remaining are A and C	55	Options remaining are A and C
37	Options remaining are C and D	56	Options remaining are B and C

£32,000

1	Options remaining are C and D	21	Options remaining are A and B
2	Options remaining are A and C	22	Options remaining are B and D
3	Options remaining are B and C	23	Options remaining are A and B
4	Options remaining are A and B	24	Options remaining are C and D
5	Options remaining are A and C	25	Options remaining are B and C
6	Options remaining are A and D	26	Options remaining are A and B
7	Options remaining are A and C	27	Options remaining are B and C
8	Options remaining are B and C	28	Options remaining are B and D
9	Options remaining are A and B	29	Options remaining are A and B
10	Options remaining are B and C	30	Options remaining are A and B
11	Options remaining are A and B	31	Options remaining are B and C
12	Options remaining are A and C	32	Options remaining are A and D
13	Options remaining are A and D	33	Options remaining are B and D
14	Options remaining are A and B	34	Options remaining are B and C
15	Options remaining are C and D	35	Options remaining are B and C
16	Options remaining are A and B	36	Options remaining are A and B
17	Options remaining are B and D	37	Options remaining are B and D
18	Options remaining are A and B	38	Options remaining are A and D
19	Options remaining are C and D	39	Options remaining are A and B
20	Options remaining are A and B	40	Options remaining are A and B

50:50

41 Options remaining are B and C	47 Options remaining are B and D
42 Options remaining are A and C	48 Options remaining are B and C
43 Options remaining are A and D	49 Options remaining are B and D
44 Options remaining are B and C	50 Options remaining are A and C
45 Options remaining are C and D	51 Options remaining are B and C
46 Options remaining are A and D	52 Options remaining are C and D

£64,000

1 Options remaining are B and C	25 Options remaining are A and D
2 Options remaining are B and C	26 Options remaining are B and C
3 Options remaining are B and C	27 Options remaining are A and C
4 Options remaining are A and D	28 Options remaining are B and D
5 Options remaining are A and B	29 Options remaining are B and C
6 Options remaining are A and C	30 Options remaining are A and D
7 Options remaining are B and C	31 Options remaining are A and B
8 Options remaining are A and D	32 Options remaining are B and C
9 Options remaining are C and D	33 Options remaining are A and D
10 Options remaining are C and D	34 Options remaining are B and D
11 Options remaining are C and D	35 Options remaining are C and D
12 Options remaining are B and C	36 Options remaining are B and C
13 Options remaining are B and D	37 Options remaining are A and C
14 Options remaining are C and D	38 Options remaining are A and B
15 Options remaining are B and D	39 Options remaining are B and D
16 Options remaining are A and D	40 Options remaining are B and D
17 Options remaining are B and D	41 Options remaining are A and C
18 Options remaining are B and D	42 Options remaining are B and C
19 Options remaining are B and C	43 Options remaining are A and B
20 Options remaining are B and C	44 Options remaining are A and B
21 Options remaining are A and B	45 Options remaining are B and D
22 Options remaining are A and B	46 Options remaining are A and C
23 Options remaining are A and D	47 Options remaining are B and D
24 Options remaining are A and B	48 Options remaining are A and D

£125,000

1 Options remaining are B and C	6 Options remaining are A and B
2 Options remaining are A and C	7 Options remaining are A and B
3 Options remaining are C and D	8 Options remaining are B and C
4 Options remaining are A and B	9 Options remaining are B and C
5 Options remaining are C and D	10 Options remaining are A and D

50:50

11	Options remaining are A and B	28	Options remaining are B and C
12	Options remaining are B and C	29	Options remaining are A and C
13	Options remaining are A and B	30	Options remaining are B and C
14	Options remaining are B and D	31	Options remaining are B and C
15	Options remaining are B and C	32	Options remaining are B and D
16	Options remaining are B and C	33	Options remaining are B and D
17	Options remaining are A and D	34	Options remaining are A and C
18	Options remaining are A and C	35	Options remaining are B and C
19	Options remaining are A and C	36	Options remaining are B and C
20	Options remaining are A and D	37	Options remaining are B and C
21	Options remaining are A and B	38	Options remaining are B and C
22	Options remaining are A and B	39	Options remaining are A and C
23	Options remaining are A and B	40	Options remaining are A and B
24	Options remaining are A and B	41	Options remaining are B and C
25	Options remaining are A and B	42	Options remaining are A and C
26	Options remaining are C and D	43	Options remaining are C and D
27	Options remaining are B and D	44	Options remaining are A and C

£250,000

1	Options remaining are B and C	21	Options remaining are C and D
2	Options remaining are A and C	22	Options remaining are B and D
3	Options remaining are A and C	23	Options remaining are A and C
4	Options remaining are B and C	24	Options remaining are A and B
5	Options remaining are A and B	25	Options remaining are A and B
6	Options remaining are A and B	26	Options remaining are B and D
7	Options remaining are B and C	27	Options remaining are A and C
8	Options remaining are B and C	28	Options remaining are A and B
9	Options remaining are B and C	29	Options remaining are B and D
10	Options remaining are A and B	30	Options remaining are A and B
11	Options remaining are A and C	31	Options remaining are A and B
12	Options remaining are A and B	32	Options remaining are A and B
13	Options remaining are A and C	33	Options remaining are C and D
14	Options remaining are B and C	34	Options remaining are A and B
15	Options remaining are A and D	35	Options remaining are A and B
16	Options remaining are B and C	36	Options remaining are B and C
17	Options remaining are B and C	37	Options remaining are B and D
18	Options remaining are A and D	38	Options remaining are A and C
19	Options remaining are C and D	39	Options remaining are A and C
20	Options remaining are B and C	40	Options remaining are C and D

50:50

£500,000

1	Options remaining are B and C	19	Options remaining are A and C
2	Options remaining are A and C	20	Options remaining are A and C
3	Options remaining are C and D	21	Options remaining are B and C
4	Options remaining are A and C	22	Options remaining are C and D
5	Options remaining are B and D	23	Options remaining are A and B
6	Options remaining are B and D	24	Options remaining are B and C
7	Options remaining are A and B	25	Options remaining are A and C
8	Options remaining are A and D	26	Options remaining are A and C
9	Options remaining are A and B	27	Options remaining are A and C
10	Options remaining are B and C	28	Options remaining are B and D
11	Options remaining are C and D	29	Options remaining are C and D
12	Options remaining are A and B	30	Options remaining are A and C
13	Options remaining are B and D	31	Options remaining are A and D
14	Options remaining are B and C	32	Options remaining are B and D
15	Options remaining are A and D	33	Options remaining are A and D
16	Options remaining are A and B	34	Options remaining are A and B
17	Options remaining are B and C	35	Options remaining are B and D
18	Options remaining are A and C	36	Options remaining are C and D

£1,000,000

1	Options remaining are B and C	17	Options remaining are A and B
2	Options remaining are A and B	18	Options remaining are A and C
3	Options remaining are A and D	19	Options remaining are B and C
4	Options remaining are C and D	20	Options remaining are B and C
5	Options remaining are A and D	21	Options remaining are A and C
6	Options remaining are A and B	22	Options remaining are A and C
7	Options remaining are C and D	23	Options remaining are A and C
8	Options remaining are A and B	24	Options remaining are C and D
9	Options remaining are B and C	25	Options remaining are C and D
10	Options remaining are A and D	26	Options remaining are B and D
11	Options remaining are A and D	27	Options remaining are B and C
12	Options remaining are B and C	28	Options remaining are C and D
13	Options remaining are A and B	29	Options remaining are A and B
14	Options remaining are A and D	30	Options remaining are A and C
15	Options remaining are A and B	31	Options remaining are B and C
16	Options remaining are C and D	32	Options remaining are B and C

Ask The Audience

£100

#	A	B	C	D		#	A	B	C	D
1	A:0%	B:16%	C:0%	D:84%		38	A:5%	B:0%	C:3%	D:92%
2	A:1%	B:11%	C:5%	D:83%		39	A:0%	B:0%	C:0%	D:100%
3	A:96%	B:4%	C:0%	D:0%		40	A:94%	B:1%	C:1%	D:4%
4	A:98%	B:0%	C:2%	D:0%		41	A:5%	B:11%	C:5%	D:79%
5	A:1%	B:2%	C:96%	D:1%		42	A:0%	B:0%	C:5%	D:95%
6	A:0%	B:95%	C:0%	D:5%		43	A:0%	B:0%	C:94%	D:6%
7	A:0%	B:0%	C:100%	D:0%		44	A:0%	B:89%	C:0%	D:11%
8	A:7%	B:93%	C:0%	D:0%		45	A:0%	B:0%	C:100%	D:0%
9	A:0%	B:100%	C:0%	D:0%		46	A:0%	B:0%	C:0%	D:100%
10	A:100%	B:0%	C:0%	D:0%		47	A:7%	B:88%	C:4%	D:1%
11	A:89%	B:0%	C:6%	D:5%		48	A:0%	B:5%	C:92%	D:3%
12	A:0%	B:0%	C:100%	D:0%		49	A:100%	B:0%	C:0%	D:0%
13	A:0%	B:0%	C:0%	D:100%		50	A:100%	B:0%	C:0%	D:0%
14	A:74%	B:26%	C:0%	D:0%		51	A:6%	B:94%	C:0%	D:0%
15	A:95%	B:0%	C:5%	D:0%		52	A:89%	B:11%	C:0%	D:0%
16	A:0%	B:100%	C:0%	D:0%		53	A:0%	B:15%	C:1%	D:84%
17	A:0%	B:0%	C:100%	D:0%		54	A:100%	B:0%	C:0%	D:0%
18	A:0%	B:0%	C:0%	D:100%		55	A:16%	B:0%	C:5%	D:79%
19	A:5%	B:5%	C:74%	D:16%		56	A:11%	B:0%	C:89%	D:0%
20	A:95%	B:0%	C:0%	D:5%		57	A:0%	B:0%	C:96%	D:4%
21	A:0%	B:0%	C:95%	D:5%		58	A:100%	B:0%	C:0%	D:0%
22	A:5%	B:16%	C:79%	D:0%		59	A:0%	B:0%	C:0%	D:100%
23	A:0%	B:100%	C:0%	D:0%		60	A:0%	B:95%	C:5%	D:0%
24	A:0%	B:100%	C:0%	D:0%		61	A:0%	B:100%	C:0%	D:0%
25	A:0%	B:5%	C:79%	D:16%		62	A:89%	B:5%	C:0%	D:6%
26	A:5%	B:5%	C:90%	D:0%		63	A:91%	B:7%	C:2%	D:0%
27	A:100%	B:0%	C:0%	D:0%		64	A:0%	B:0%	C:0%	D:100%
28	A:100%	B:0%	C:0%	D:0%		65	A:0%	B:1%	C:6%	D:93%
29	A:100%	B:0%	C:0%	D:0%		66	A:0%	B:0%	C:100%	D:0%
30	A:91%	B:6%	C:3%	D:0%		67	A:0%	B:0%	C:100%	D:0%
31	A:0%	B:0%	C:100%	D:0%		68	A:0%	B:0%	C:0%	D:100%
32	A:0%	B:0%	C:100%	D:0%		69	A:100%	B:0%	C:0%	D:0%
33	A:0%	B:100%	C:0%	D:0%		70	A:0%	B:100%	C:0%	D:0%
34	A:95%	B:0%	C:0%	D:5%		71	A:0%	B:0%	C:100%	D:0%
35	A:5%	B:0%	C:86%	D:9%		72	A:5%	B:16%	C:0%	D:79%
36	A:0%	B:5%	C:16%	D:79%		73	A:4%	B:95%	C:1%	D:0%
37	A:0%	B:100%	C:0%	D:0%		74	A:5%	B:0%	C:94%	D:1%

ASK THE AUDIENCE

75	A:0%	B:0%	C:0%	D:100%	82	A:0%	B:0%	C:89%	D:11%
76	A:5%	B:95%	C:0%	D:0%	83	A:0%	B:0%	C:100%	D:0%
77	A:3%	B:3%	C:4%	D:90%	84	A:95%	B:0%	C:5%	D:0%
78	A:94%	B:6%	C:0%	D:0%	85	A:11%	B:5%	C:74%	D:10%
79	A:0%	B:0%	C:100%	D:0%	86	A:100%	B:0%	C:0%	D:0%
80	A:100%	B:0%	C:0%	D:0%	87	A:0%	B:84%	C:16%	D:0%
81	A:5%	B:87%	C:7%	D:1%	88	A:9%	B:2%	C:89%	D:0%

£200

1	A:100%	B:0%	C:0%	D:0%	33	A:0%	B:0%	C:100%	D:0%
2	A:0%	B:100%	C:0%	D:0%	34	A:79%	B:11%	C:5%	D:5%
3	A:0%	B:6%	C:92%	D:2%	35	A:0%	B:0%	C:100%	D:0%
4	A:100%	B:0%	C:0%	D:0%	36	A:0%	B:100%	C:0%	D:0%
5	A:4%	B:0%	C:0%	D:96%	37	A:5%	B:0%	C:95%	D:0%
6	A:0%	B:100%	C:0%	D:0%	38	A:12%	B:0%	C:86%	D:2%
7	A:0%	B:5%	C:0%	D:95%	39	A:0%	B:89%	C:11%	D:0%
8	A:6%	B:0%	C:68%	D:26%	40	A:100%	B:0%	C:0%	D:0%
9	A:100%	B:0%	C:0%	D:0%	41	A:42%	B:0%	C:53%	D:5%
10	A:5%	B:7%	C:84%	D:4%	42	A:0%	B:2%	C:87%	D:11%
11	A:100%	B:0%	C:0%	D:0%	43	A:100%	B:0%	C:0%	D:0%
12	A:16%	B:5%	C:77%	D:2%	44	A:89%	B:0%	C:6%	D:5%
13	A:5%	B:79%	C:16%	D:0%	45	A:100%	B:0%	C:0%	D:0%
14	A:5%	B:0%	C:95%	D:0%	46	A:0%	B:100%	C:0%	D:0%
15	A:5%	B:5%	C:83%	D:7%	47	A:0%	B:0%	C:0%	D:100%
16	A:5%	B:85%	C:0%	D:10%	48	A:5%	B:0%	C:91%	D:4%
17	A:0%	B:95%	C:0%	D:5%	49	A:7%	B:89%	C:4%	D:0%
18	A:11%	B:5%	C:84%	D:0%	50	A:13%	B:0%	C:0%	D:87%
19	A:89%	B:9%	C:2%	D:0%	51	A:2%	B:2%	C:91%	D:5%
20	A:0%	B:5%	C:0%	D:95%	52	A:26%	B:11%	C:5%	D:58%
21	A:0%	B:100%	C:0%	D:0%	53	A:4%	B:0%	C:96%	D:0%
22	A:11%	B:10%	C:5%	D:74%	54	A:0%	B:0%	C:100%	D:0%
23	A:5%	B:87%	C:1%	D:7%	55	A:21%	B:63%	C:11%	D:5%
24	A:89%	B:0%	C:0%	D:11%	56	A:0%	B:0%	C:100%	D:0%
25	A:5%	B:84%	C:0%	D:11%	57	A:37%	B:58%	C:0%	D:5%
26	A:21%	B:16%	C:63%	D:0%	58	A:5%	B:0%	C:84%	D:11%
27	A:0%	B:5%	C:6%	D:89%	59	A:11%	B:0%	C:0%	D:89%
28	A:0%	B:0%	C:95%	D:5%	60	A:5%	B:6%	C:84%	D:5%
29	A:0%	B:5%	C:91%	D:4%	61	A:0%	B:0%	C:95%	D:5%
30	A:6%	B:1%	C:93%	D:0%	62	A:68%	B:16%	C:5%	D:11%
31	A:68%	B:5%	C:11%	D:16%	63	A:0%	B:0%	C:100%	D:0%
32	A:5%	B:6%	C:26%	D:63%	64	A:0%	B:95%	C:0%	D:5%

ASK THE AUDIENCE

65	A:0%	B:100%	C:0%	D:0%
66	A:0%	B:47%	C:42%	D:11%
67	A:89%	B:5%	C:6%	D:0%
68	A:0%	B:0%	C:5%	D:95%
69	A:0%	B:95%	C:5%	D:0%
70	A:92%	B:3%	C:0%	D:5%
71	A:100%	B:0%	C:0%	D:0%
72	A:16%	B:5%	C:5%	D:74%
73	A:95%	B:5%	C:0%	D:0%
74	A:4%	B:7%	C:5%	D:84%
75	A:5%	B:68%	C:6%	D:21%
76	A:16%	B:0%	C:79%	D:5%
77	A:32%	B:21%	C:5%	D:42%
78	A:5%	B:5%	C:90%	D:0%
79	A:95%	B:0%	C:0%	D:5%
80	A:7%	B:2%	C:91%	D:0%
81	A:5%	B:89%	C:6%	D:0%
82	A:0%	B:5%	C:0%	D:95%
83	A:21%	B:79%	C:0%	D:0%
84	A:94%	B:5%	C:1%	D:0%

£300

1	A:5%	B:42%	C:32%	D:21%
2	A:89%	B:0%	C:2%	D:9%
3	A:11%	B:21%	C:0%	D:68%
4	A:5%	B:84%	C:0%	D:11%
5	A:0%	B:5%	C:0%	D:95%
6	A:26%	B:63%	C:6%	D:5%
7	A:2%	B:93%	C:5%	D:0%
8	A:5%	B:85%	C:7%	D:3%
9	A:0%	B:6%	C:89%	D:5%
10	A:5%	B:0%	C:0%	D:95%
11	A:11%	B:89%	C:0%	D:0%
12	A:0%	B:16%	C:47%	D:37%
13	A:0%	B:100%	C:0%	D:0%
14	A:5%	B:74%	C:16%	D:5%
15	A:100%	B:0%	C:0%	D:0%
16	A:0%	B:100%	C:0%	D:0%
17	A:5%	B:95%	C:0%	D:0%
18	A:95%	B:0%	C:0%	D:5%
19	A:0%	B:100%	C:0%	D:0%
20	A:0%	B:95%	C:5%	D:0%
21	A:0%	B:5%	C:5%	D:90%
22	A:16%	B:0%	C:84%	D:0%
23	A:5%	B:0%	C:32%	D:63%
24	A:5%	B:0%	C:95%	D:0%
25	A:32%	B:16%	C:47%	D:5%
26	A:8%	B:2%	C:16%	D:74%
27	A:16%	B:84%	C:0%	D:0%
28	A:16%	B:0%	C:79%	D:5%
29	A:11%	B:84%	C:0%	D:5%
30	A:6%	B:87%	C:7%	D:0%
31	A:5%	B:95%	C:0%	D:0%
32	A:5%	B:89%	C:1%	D:5%
33	A:0%	B:5%	C:94%	D:1%
34	A:11%	B:84%	C:5%	D:0%
35	A:0%	B:0%	C:100%	D:0%
36	A:0%	B:5%	C:84%	D:11%
37	A:34%	B:42%	C:8%	D:16%
38	A:21%	B:0%	C:5%	D:74%
39	A:5%	B:10%	C:74%	D:11%
40	A:0%	B:0%	C:100%	D:0%
41	A:5%	B:11%	C:0%	D:84%
42	A:5%	B:95%	C:0%	D:0%
43	A:5%	B:11%	C:5%	D:79%
44	A:5%	B:0%	C:0%	D:95%
45	A:21%	B:58%	C:9%	D:12%
46	A:58%	B:21%	C:5%	D:16%
47	A:100%	B:0%	C:0%	D:0%
48	A:5%	B:0%	C:95%	D:0%
49	A:16%	B:26%	C:58%	D:0%
50	A:0%	B:5%	C:0%	D:95%
51	A:1%	B:6%	C:0%	D:93%
52	A:0%	B:16%	C:84%	D:0%
53	A:84%	B:5%	C:11%	D:0%
54	A:95%	B:5%	C:0%	D:0%
55	A:100%	B:0%	C:0%	D:0%
56	A:0%	B:89%	C:11%	D:0%
57	A:5%	B:7%	C:4%	D:84%
58	A:100%	B:0%	C:0%	D:0%

ASK THE AUDIENCE

59	A:0%	B:0%	C:100%	D:0%	70	A:42%	B:0%	C:0%	D:58%
60	A:6%	B:87%	C:7%	D:0%	71	A:2%	B:91%	C:2%	D:5%
61	A:74%	B:0%	C:21%	D:5%	72	A:0%	B:0%	C:100%	D:0%
62	A:16%	B:79%	C:5%	D:0%	73	A:0%	B:0%	C:100%	D:0%
63	A:0%	B:100%	C:0%	D:0%	74	A:6%	B:89%	C:5%	D:0%
64	A:5%	B:6%	C:0%	D:89%	75	A:32%	B:53%	C:4%	D:11%
65	A:100%	B:0%	C:0%	D:0%	76	A:0%	B:5%	C:95%	D:0%
66	A:0%	B:0%	C:100%	D:0%	77	A:89%	B:11%	C:0%	D:0%
67	A:0%	B:100%	C:0%	D:0%	78	A:0%	B:0%	C:0%	D:100%
68	A:100%	B:0%	C:0%	D:0%	79	A:0%	B:0%	C:100%	D:0%
69	A:95%	B:5%	C:0%	D:0%	80	A:42%	B:37%	C:9%	D:12%

£500

1	A:0%	B:100%	C:0%	D:0%	28	A:11%	B:16%	C:68%	D:5%
2	A:0%	B:0%	C:100%	D:0%	29	A:26%	B:68%	C:6%	D:0%
3	A:100%	B:0%	C:0%	D:0%	30	A:9%	B:1%	C:74%	D:16%
4	A:0%	B:0%	C:0%	D:100%	31	A:0%	B:95%	C:0%	D:5%
5	A:97%	B:0%	C:0%	D:3%	32	A:5%	B:0%	C:95%	D:0%
6	A:0%	B:1%	C:5%	D:94%	33	A:0%	B:11%	C:10%	D:79%
7	A:95%	B:0%	C:0%	D:5%	34	A:0%	B:0%	C:100%	D:0%
8	A:0%	B:0%	C:0%	D:100%	35	A:2%	B:87%	C:6%	D:5%
9	A:0%	B:16%	C:84%	D:0%	36	A:0%	B:0%	C:5%	D:95%
10	A:0%	B:0%	C:0%	D:100%	37	A:5%	B:89%	C:6%	D:0%
11	A:0%	B:93%	C:2%	D:5%	38	A:89%	B:0%	C:0%	D:11%
12	A:100%	B:0%	C:0%	D:0%	39	A:6%	B:4%	C:90%	D:0%
13	A:0%	B:100%	C:0%	D:0%	40	A:100%	B:0%	C:0%	D:0%
14	A:5%	B:74%	C:16%	D:5%	41	A:10%	B:74%	C:0%	D:16%
15	A:5%	B:11%	C:84%	D:0%	42	A:0%	B:0%	C:0%	D:100%
16	A:0%	B:0%	C:100%	D:0%	43	A:0%	B:0%	C:100%	D:0%
17	A:8%	B:4%	C:1%	D:87%	44	A:100%	B:0%	C:0%	D:0%
18	A:5%	B:95%	C:0%	D:0%	45	A:0%	B:0%	C:95%	D:5%
19	A:21%	B:58%	C:9%	D:12%	46	A:0%	B:0%	C:0%	D:100%
20	A:84%	B:11%	C:0%	D:5%	47	A:0%	B:0%	C:5%	D:95%
21	A:0%	B:0%	C:0%	D:100%	48	A:5%	B:42%	C:32%	D:21%
22	A:0%	B:0%	C:100%	D:0%	49	A:12%	B:4%	C:5%	D:79%
23	A:0%	B:11%	C:89%	D:0%	50	A:0%	B:11%	C:84%	D:5%
24	A:84%	B:16%	C:0%	D:0%	51	A:9%	B:53%	C:6%	D:32%
25	A:6%	B:88%	C:6%	D:0%	52	A:16%	B:0%	C:10%	D:74%
26	A:0%	B:5%	C:0%	D:95%	53	A:0%	B:5%	C:0%	D:95%
27	A:0%	B:100%	C:0%	D:0%	54	A:100%	B:0%	C:0%	D:0%

ASK THE AUDIENCE

55	A:11%	B:5%	C:5%	D:79%	66	A:100%	B:0%	C:0%	D:0%
56	A:95%	B:5%	C:0%	D:0%	67	A:0%	B:100%	C:0%	D:0%
57	A:0%	B:68%	C:0%	D:32%	68	A:21%	B:5%	C:0%	D:74%
58	A:16%	B:84%	C:0%	D:0%	69	A:0%	B:94%	C:6%	D:0%
59	A:0%	B:4%	C:91%	D:5%	70	A:0%	B:0%	C:74%	D:26%
60	A:0%	B:0%	C:0%	D:100%	71	A:100%	B:0%	C:0%	D:0%
61	A:0%	B:0%	C:0%	D:100%	72	A:89%	B:0%	C:11%	D:0%
62	A:0%	B:100%	C:0%	D:0%	73	A:11%	B:0%	C:0%	D:89%
63	A:5%	B:79%	C:5%	D:11%	74	A:26%	B:12%	C:42%	D:20%
64	A:11%	B:68%	C:12%	D:9%	75	A:16%	B:15%	C:11%	D:58%
65	A:95%	B:0%	C:5%	D:0%	76	A:0%	B:0%	C:0%	D:100%

£1,000

1	A:0%	B:5%	C:1%	D:94%	29	A:1%	B:86%	C:8%	D:5%
2	A:0%	B:100%	C:0%	D:0%	30	A:12%	B:88%	C:0%	D:0%
3	A:0%	B:0%	C:100%	D:0%	31	A:0%	B:0%	C:100%	D:0%
4	A:89%	B:6%	C:0%	D:5%	32	A:0%	B:0%	C:5%	D:95%
5	A:5%	B:90%	C:5%	D:0%	33	A:0%	B:100%	C:0%	D:0%
6	A:0%	B:10%	C:16%	D:74%	34	A:11%	B:10%	C:5%	D:74%
7	A:0%	B:0%	C:100%	D:0%	35	A:5%	B:1%	C:87%	D:7%
8	A:0%	B:95%	C:0%	D:5%	36	A:2%	B:9%	C:0%	D:89%
9	A:5%	B:0%	C:93%	D:2%	37	A:11%	B:5%	C:84%	D:0%
10	A:0%	B:5%	C:95%	D:0%	38	A:0%	B:0%	C:100%	D:0%
11	A:6%	B:94%	C:0%	D:0%	39	A:0%	B:4%	C:90%	D:6%
12	A:5%	B:90%	C:0%	D:5%	40	A:7%	B:4%	C:89%	D:0%
13	A:16%	B:20%	C:11%	D:53%	41	A:5%	B:74%	C:5%	D:16%
14	A:11%	B:89%	C:0%	D:0%	42	A:5%	B:11%	C:68%	D:16%
15	A:5%	B:84%	C:7%	D:4%	43	A:0%	B:26%	C:53%	D:21%
16	A:5%	B:95%	C:0%	D:0%	44	A:19%	B:21%	C:23%	D:37%
17	A:42%	B:37%	C:11%	D:10%	45	A:0%	B:100%	C:0%	D:0%
18	A:5%	B:11%	C:5%	D:79%	46	A:0%	B:0%	C:0%	D:100%
19	A:0%	B:95%	C:5%	D:0%	47	A:0%	B:0%	C:63%	D:37%
20	A:5%	B:0%	C:11%	D:84%	48	A:0%	B:89%	C:11%	D:0%
21	A:6%	B:94%	C:0%	D:0%	49	A:16%	B:84%	C:0%	D:0%
22	A:16%	B:58%	C:21%	D:5%	50	A:0%	B:0%	C:100%	D:0%
23	A:95%	B:0%	C:0%	D:5%	51	A:4%	B:7%	C:84%	D:5%
24	A:95%	B:5%	C:0%	D:0%	52	A:16%	B:79%	C:0%	D:5%
25	A:16%	B:11%	C:68%	D:5%	53	A:26%	B:11%	C:0%	D:63%
26	A:100%	B:0%	C:0%	D:0%	54	A:16%	B:74%	C:10%	D:0%
27	A:5%	B:0%	C:6%	D:89%	55	A:5%	B:47%	C:0%	D:48%
28	A:21%	B:63%	C:5%	D:11%	56	A:16%	B:63%	C:16%	D:5%

ASK THE AUDIENCE

57	A:5%	B:5%	C:11%	D:79%	65	A:12%	B:9%	C:63%	D:16%
58	A:5%	B:1%	C:88%	D:6%	66	A:11%	B:63%	C:21%	D:5%
59	A:5%	B:6%	C:79%	D:10%	67	A:16%	B:37%	C:42%	D:5%
60	A:84%	B:9%	C:7%	D:0%	68	A:5%	B:32%	C:42%	D:21%
61	A:6%	B:0%	C:5%	D:89%	69	A:1%	B:4%	C:6%	D:89%
62	A:26%	B:11%	C:58%	D:5%	70	A:58%	B:21%	C:5%	D:16%
63	A:26%	B:63%	C:8%	D:3%	71	A:2%	B:5%	C:6%	D:87%
64	A:79%	B:16%	C:5%	D:0%	72	A:5%	B:84%	C:4%	D:7%

£2,000

1	A:10%	B:47%	C:11%	D:32%	32	A:79%	B:5%	C:16%	D:0%
2	A:47%	B:9%	C:2%	D:42%	33	A:5%	B:74%	C:10%	D:11%
3	A:12%	B:68%	C:4%	D:16%	34	A:4%	B:89%	C:0%	D:7%
4	A:79%	B:5%	C:7%	D:9%	35	A:26%	B:47%	C:16%	D:11%
5	A:0%	B:100%	C:0%	D:0%	36	A:10%	B:6%	C:0%	D:84%
6	A:68%	B:16%	C:15%	D:1%	37	A:21%	B:5%	C:58%	D:16%
7	A:95%	B:5%	C:0%	D:0%	38	A:89%	B:7%	C:3%	D:1%
8	A:0%	B:11%	C:79%	D:10%	39	A:89%	B:5%	C:6%	D:0%
9	A:82%	B:8%	C:6%	D:4%	40	A:11%	B:10%	C:79%	D:0%
10	A:89%	B:0%	C:0%	D:11%	41	A:6%	B:26%	C:0%	D:68%
11	A:32%	B:42%	C:21%	D:5%	42	A:11%	B:89%	C:0%	D:0%
12	A:16%	B:0%	C:5%	D:79%	43	A:58%	B:37%	C:5%	D:0%
13	A:84%	B:5%	C:6%	D:5%	44	A:0%	B:5%	C:89%	D:6%
14	A:0%	B:84%	C:13%	D:3%	45	A:7%	B:4%	C:10%	D:79%
15	A:10%	B:0%	C:11%	D:79%	46	A:6%	B:89%	C:5%	D:0%
16	A:12%	B:0%	C:2%	D:86%	47	A:3%	B:1%	C:94%	D:2%
17	A:11%	B:79%	C:2%	D:8%	48	A:5%	B:95%	C:0%	D:0%
18	A:11%	B:84%	C:5%	D:0%	49	A:47%	B:11%	C:5%	D:37%
19	A:16%	B:5%	C:79%	D:0%	50	A:95%	B:0%	C:0%	D:5%
20	A:5%	B:0%	C:6%	D:89%	51	A:5%	B:0%	C:95%	D:0%
21	A:16%	B:79%	C:2%	D:3%	52	A:0%	B:42%	C:26%	D:32%
22	A:16%	B:0%	C:5%	D:79%	53	A:63%	B:0%	C:26%	D:11%
23	A:6%	B:5%	C:89%	D:0%	54	A:0%	B:16%	C:84%	D:0%
24	A:4%	B:95%	C:1%	D:0%	55	A:21%	B:63%	C:13%	D:3%
25	A:5%	B:14%	C:0%	D:81%	56	A:5%	B:84%	C:0%	D:11%
26	A:21%	B:0%	C:68%	D:11%	57	A:6%	B:5%	C:84%	D:5%
27	A:67%	B:16%	C:7%	D:10%	58	A:0%	B:100%	C:0%	D:0%
28	A:16%	B:5%	C:68%	D:11%	59	A:13%	B:79%	C:3%	D:5%
29	A:16%	B:16%	C:68%	D:0%	60	A:11%	B:5%	C:68%	D:16%
30	A:11%	B:15%	C:0%	D:74%	61	A:5%	B:95%	C:0%	D:0%
31	A:21%	B:74%	C:0%	D:5%	62	A:0%	B:84%	C:5%	D:11%

ASK THE AUDIENCE

63	A:63%	B:5%	C:16%	D:16%	66	A:5%	B:58%	C:31%	D:6%
64	A:26%	B:21%	C:42%	D:11%	67	A:3%	B:12%	C:74%	D:11%
65	A:21%	B:11%	C:47%	D:21%	68	A:26%	B:58%	C:16%	D:0%

£4,000

1	A:0%	B:100%	C:0%	D:0%	33	A:21%	B:21%	C:16%	D:42%
2	A:42%	B:26%	C:32%	D:0%	34	A:12%	B:4%	C:47%	D:37%
3	A:63%	B:16%	C:5%	D:16%	35	A:5%	B:0%	C:95%	D:0%
4	A:58%	B:5%	C:11%	D:26%	36	A:26%	B:0%	C:63%	D:11%
5	A:21%	B:0%	C:74%	D:5%	37	A:0%	B:0%	C:0%	D:100%
6	A:84%	B:5%	C:11%	D:0%	38	A:95%	B:0%	C:0%	D:5%
7	A:53%	B:41%	C:0%	D:6%	39	A:84%	B:7%	C:3%	D:6%
8	A:32%	B:5%	C:63%	D:0%	40	A:11%	B:68%	C:0%	D:21%
9	A:89%	B:5%	C:5%	D:1%	41	A:0%	B:11%	C:84%	D:5%
10	A:68%	B:16%	C:7%	D:9%	42	A:79%	B:0%	C:11%	D:10%
11	A:0%	B:37%	C:16%	D:47%	43	A:0%	B:0%	C:74%	D:26%
12	A:11%	B:21%	C:21%	D:47%	44	A:21%	B:68%	C:5%	D:6%
13	A:16%	B:26%	C:58%	D:0%	45	A:5%	B:58%	C:16%	D:21%
14	A:4%	B:11%	C:32%	D:53%	46	A:74%	B:0%	C:5%	D:21%
15	A:11%	B:21%	C:58%	D:10%	47	A:63%	B:8%	C:13%	D:16%
16	A:74%	B:12%	C:6%	D:8%	48	A:58%	B:10%	C:11%	D:21%
17	A:89%	B:0%	C:0%	D:11%	49	A:11%	B:32%	C:53%	D:4%
18	A:100%	B:0%	C:0%	D:0%	50	A:37%	B:32%	C:31%	D:0%
19	A:32%	B:58%	C:5%	D:5%	51	A:68%	B:16%	C:11%	D:5%
20	A:89%	B:1%	C:7%	D:3%	52	A:3%	B:0%	C:84%	D:13%
21	A:11%	B:21%	C:63%	D:5%	53	A:32%	B:22%	C:20%	D:26%
22	A:42%	B:21%	C:0%	D:37%	54	A:6%	B:89%	C:0%	D:5%
23	A:100%	B:0%	C:0%	D:0%	55	A:89%	B:11%	C:0%	D:0%
24	A:9%	B:16%	C:63%	D:12%	56	A:5%	B:6%	C:85%	D:4%
25	A:11%	B:84%	C:5%	D:0%	57	A:63%	B:21%	C:11%	D:5%
26	A:100%	B:0%	C:0%	D:0%	58	A:11%	B:0%	C:79%	D:10%
27	A:9%	B:12%	C:5%	D:74%	59	A:15%	B:84%	C:0%	D:1%
28	A:10%	B:16%	C:74%	D:0%	60	A:16%	B:12%	C:63%	D:9%
29	A:1%	B:16%	C:74%	D:9%	61	A:5%	B:11%	C:74%	D:10%
30	A:21%	B:58%	C:0%	D:21%	62	A:21%	B:26%	C:16%	D:37%
31	A:5%	B:11%	C:0%	D:84%	63	A:95%	B:0%	C:0%	D:5%
32	A:74%	B:16%	C:0%	D:10%	64	A:21%	B:11%	C:68%	D:0%

ASK THE AUDIENCE

£8,000

#	A	B	C	D	#	A	B	C	D
1	A:11%	B:5%	C:84%	D:0%	31	A:8%	B:16%	C:63%	D:13%
2	A:7%	B:47%	C:41%	D:5%	32	A:11%	B:84%	C:0%	D:5%
3	A:89%	B:5%	C:0%	D:6%	33	A:68%	B:5%	C:1%	D:26%
4	A:16%	B:21%	C:32%	D:31%	34	A:5%	B:58%	C:26%	D:11%
5	A:68%	B:4%	C:16%	D:12%	35	A:5%	B:85%	C:4%	D:6%
6	A:26%	B:58%	C:11%	D:5%	36	A:16%	B:21%	C:63%	D:0%
7	A:16%	B:21%	C:16%	D:47%	37	A:95%	B:5%	C:0%	D:0%
8	A:21%	B:5%	C:53%	D:21%	38	A:5%	B:68%	C:16%	D:11%
9	A:3%	B:13%	C:79%	D:5%	39	A:0%	B:16%	C:79%	D:5%
10	A:11%	B:21%	C:0%	D:68%	40	A:5%	B:79%	C:11%	D:5%
11	A:53%	B:37%	C:5%	D:5%	41	A:32%	B:5%	C:42%	D:21%
12	A:11%	B:5%	C:84%	D:0%	42	A:16%	B:26%	C:47%	D:11%
13	A:6%	B:0%	C:89%	D:5%	43	A:5%	B:1%	C:68%	D:26%
14	A:5%	B:84%	C:11%	D:0%	44	A:42%	B:32%	C:10%	D:16%
15	A:16%	B:74%	C:5%	D:5%	45	A:0%	B:0%	C:5%	D:95%
16	A:5%	B:74%	C:16%	D:5%	46	A:32%	B:42%	C:14%	D:12%
17	A:26%	B:16%	C:5%	D:53%	47	A:11%	B:32%	C:47%	D:10%
18	A:21%	B:47%	C:10%	D:22%	48	A:12%	B:33%	C:45%	D:10%
19	A:16%	B:11%	C:68%	D:5%	49	A:0%	B:0%	C:100%	D:0%
20	A:5%	B:89%	C:6%	D:0%	50	A:21%	B:0%	C:11%	D:68%
21	A:4%	B:63%	C:26%	D:7%	51	A:63%	B:32%	C:0%	D:5%
22	A:6%	B:5%	C:89%	D:0%	52	A:5%	B:47%	C:22%	D:26%
23	A:5%	B:0%	C:16%	D:79%	53	A:79%	B:11%	C:10%	D:0%
24	A:10%	B:11%	C:58%	D:21%	54	A:0%	B:63%	C:21%	D:16%
25	A:5%	B:95%	C:0%	D:0%	55	A:74%	B:1%	C:9%	D:16%
26	A:74%	B:9%	C:16%	D:1%	56	A:9%	B:68%	C:13%	D:10%
27	A:21%	B:53%	C:10%	D:16%	57	A:0%	B:95%	C:5%	D:0%
28	A:5%	B:6%	C:0%	D:89%	58	A:5%	B:95%	C:0%	D:0%
29	A:5%	B:84%	C:0%	D:11%	59	A:5%	B:0%	C:89%	D:6%
30	A:0%	B:100%	C:0%	D:0%	60	A:89%	B:0%	C:0%	D:11%

£16,000

#	A	B	C	D	#	A	B	C	D
1	A:5%	B:7%	C:82%	D:6%	9	A:32%	B:26%	C:37%	D:5%
2	A:89%	B:0%	C:9%	D:2%	10	A:0%	B:9%	C:89%	D:2%
3	A:1%	B:92%	C:0%	D:7%	11	A:16%	B:53%	C:16%	D:15%
4	A:95%	B:0%	C:3%	D:2%	12	A:9%	B:12%	C:63%	D:16%
5	A:11%	B:87%	C:2%	D:0%	13	A:0%	B:6%	C:89%	D:5%
6	A:58%	B:16%	C:21%	D:5%	14	A:21%	B:68%	C:11%	D:0%
7	A:5%	B:16%	C:53%	D:26%	15	A:11%	B:63%	C:21%	D:5%
8	A:0%	B:1%	C:16%	D:83%	16	A:5%	B:26%	C:68%	D:1%

ASK THE AUDIENCE

17	A:0%	B:26%	C:0%	D:74%	37	A:0%	B:0%	C:5%	D:95%
18	A:5%	B:2%	C:3%	D:90%	38	A:5%	B:0%	C:79%	D:16%
19	A:5%	B:11%	C:84%	D:0%	39	A:79%	B:11%	C:7%	D:3%
20	A:11%	B:68%	C:5%	D:16%	40	A:11%	B:63%	C:21%	D:5%
21	A:68%	B:5%	C:1%	D:26%	41	A:22%	B:2%	C:68%	D:8%
22	A:32%	B:26%	C:26%	D:16%	42	A:0%	B:100%	C:0%	D:0%
23	A:74%	B:9%	C:12%	D:5%	43	A:32%	B:1%	C:58%	D:9%
24	A:10%	B:42%	C:32%	D:16%	44	A:11%	B:68%	C:16%	D:5%
25	A:89%	B:2%	C:4%	D:5%	45	A:0%	B:89%	C:6%	D:5%
26	A:21%	B:4%	C:68%	D:7%	46	A:75%	B:13%	C:8%	D:4%
27	A:53%	B:9%	C:16%	D:22%	47	A:16%	B:68%	C:0%	D:16%
28	A:11%	B:10%	C:53%	D:26%	48	A:26%	B:47%	C:21%	D:6%
29	A:12%	B:4%	C:5%	D:79%	49	A:5%	B:89%	C:1%	D:5%
30	A:5%	B:0%	C:6%	D:89%	50	A:37%	B:42%	C:21%	D:0%
31	A:15%	B:16%	C:1%	D:68%	51	A:21%	B:20%	C:12%	D:47%
32	A:5%	B:0%	C:42%	D:53%	52	A:5%	B:11%	C:84%	D:0%
33	A:9%	B:2%	C:84%	D:5%	53	A:26%	B:42%	C:22%	D:10%
34	A:11%	B:12%	C:73%	D:4%	54	A:10%	B:5%	C:11%	D:74%
35	A:5%	B:74%	C:15%	D:6%	55	A:21%	B:26%	C:53%	D:0%
36	A:84%	B:9%	C:2%	D:5%	56	A:23%	B:9%	C:47%	D:21%

£32,000

1	A:16%	B:15%	C:53%	D:16%	20	A:63%	B:21%	C:5%	D:11%
2	A:16%	B:5%	C:74%	D:5%	21	A:68%	B:26%	C:5%	D:1%
3	A:0%	B:26%	C:63%	D:11%	22	A:5%	B:74%	C:15%	D:6%
4	A:84%	B:5%	C:9%	D:2%	23	A:7%	B:89%	C:4%	D:0%
5	A:16%	B:32%	C:26%	D:26%	24	A:16%	B:16%	C:42%	D:26%
6	A:79%	B:2%	C:8%	D:11%	25	A:26%	B:16%	C:53%	D:5%
7	A:79%	B:16%	C:0%	D:5%	26	A:32%	B:2%	C:35%	D:31%
8	A:32%	B:47%	C:12%	D:9%	27	A:5%	B:32%	C:21%	D:42%
9	A:32%	B:53%	C:5%	D:10%	28	A:16%	B:68%	C:11%	D:5%
10	A:13%	B:21%	C:61%	D:5%	29	A:5%	B:74%	C:5%	D:16%
11	A:47%	B:32%	C:21%	D:0%	30	A:21%	B:63%	C:16%	D:0%
12	A:63%	B:5%	C:11%	D:21%	31	A:0%	B:58%	C:16%	D:26%
13	A:63%	B:21%	C:16%	D:0%	32	A:47%	B:18%	C:26%	D:9%
14	A:37%	B:16%	C:38%	D:9%	33	A:16%	B:53%	C:11%	D:20%
15	A:11%	B:47%	C:16%	D:26%	34	A:16%	B:63%	C:16%	D:5%
16	A:53%	B:16%	C:26%	D:5%	35	A:6%	B:53%	C:32%	D:9%
17	A:3%	B:89%	C:2%	D:6%	36	A:0%	B:84%	C:5%	D:11%
18	A:11%	B:79%	C:9%	D:1%	37	A:42%	B:37%	C:0%	D:21%
19	A:5%	B:16%	C:5%	D:74%	38	A:32%	B:32%	C:10%	D:26%

ASK THE AUDIENCE

39	A:37%	B:26%	C:11%	D:26%
40	A:37%	B:58%	C:2%	D:3%
41	A:5%	B:85%	C:4%	D:6%
42	A:63%	B:21%	C:11%	D:5%
43	A:21%	B:33%	C:9%	D:37%
44	A:5%	B:79%	C:16%	D:0%
45	A:7%	B:9%	C:79%	D:5%

46	A:63%	B:11%	C:10%	D:16%
47	A:16%	B:32%	C:15%	D:37%
48	A:42%	B:21%	C:32%	D:5%
49	A:16%	B:58%	C:9%	D:17%
50	A:16%	B:10%	C:53%	D:21%
51	A:15%	B:11%	C:53%	D:21%
52	A:17%	B:20%	C:21%	D:42%

£64,000

1	A:21%	B:58%	C:11%	D:10%
2	A:16%	B:47%	C:21%	D:16%
3	A:0%	B:21%	C:53%	D:26%
4	A:68%	B:14%	C:16%	D:2%
5	A:42%	B:11%	C:15%	D:32%
6	A:53%	B:10%	C:21%	D:16%
7	A:0%	B:58%	C:37%	D:5%
8	A:37%	B:21%	C:23%	D:19%
9	A:12%	B:9%	C:68%	D:11%
10	A:5%	B:16%	C:74%	D:5%
11	A:5%	B:6%	C:84%	D:5%
12	A:16%	B:37%	C:26%	D:21%
13	A:16%	B:42%	C:16%	D:26%
14	A:12%	B:9%	C:63%	D:16%
15	A:5%	B:42%	C:6%	D:47%
16	A:32%	B:16%	C:32%	D:20%
17	A:5%	B:37%	C:16%	D:42%
18	A:16%	B:17%	C:9%	D:58%
19	A:5%	B:47%	C:37%	D:11%
20	A:11%	B:47%	C:21%	D:21%
21	A:21%	B:74%	C:5%	D:0%
22	A:26%	B:69%	C:2%	D:3%
23	A:11%	B:16%	C:10%	D:63%
24	A:26%	B:47%	C:14%	D:13%

25	A:47%	B:9%	C:12%	D:32%
26	A:37%	B:5%	C:52%	D:6%
27	A:10%	B:37%	C:11%	D:42%
28	A:21%	B:33%	C:9%	D:37%
29	A:16%	B:5%	C:74%	D:5%
30	A:16%	B:21%	C:42%	D:21%
31	A:16%	B:74%	C:5%	D:5%
32	A:58%	B:16%	C:13%	D:13%
33	A:32%	B:5%	C:16%	D:47%
34	A:3%	B:42%	C:2%	D:53%
35	A:10%	B:27%	C:58%	D:5%
36	A:21%	B:47%	C:26%	D:6%
37	A:86%	B:1%	C:2%	D:11%
38	A:26%	B:47%	C:5%	D:22%
39	A:13%	B:63%	C:14%	D:10%
40	A:11%	B:68%	C:5%	D:16%
41	A:58%	B:16%	C:5%	D:21%
42	A:1%	B:4%	C:89%	D:6%
43	A:37%	B:34%	C:24%	D:5%
44	A:33%	B:31%	C:28%	D:8%
45	A:26%	B:16%	C:47%	D:11%
46	A:12%	B:4%	C:68%	D:16%
47	A:21%	B:47%	C:16%	D:16%
48	A:58%	B:2%	C:19%	D:21%

£125,000

1	A:5%	B:16%	C:58%	D:21%
2	A:88%	B:5%	C:6%	D:1%
3	A:9%	B:16%	C:74%	D:1%
4	A:37%	B:53%	C:5%	D:5%

5	A:2%	B:40%	C:37%	D:21%
6	A:11%	B:32%	C:46%	D:11%
7	A:16%	B:42%	C:26%	D:16%
8	A:64%	B:31%	C:3%	D:2%

ASK THE AUDIENCE

#	A	B	C	D	#	A	B	C	D
9	A:32%	B:12%	C:47%	D:9%	27	A:3%	B:84%	C:8%	D:5%
10	A:62%	B:4%	C:13%	D:21%	28	A:32%	B:50%	C:16%	D:2%
11	A:32%	B:37%	C:11%	D:20%	29	A:21%	B:5%	C:47%	D:27%
12	A:37%	B:53%	C:4%	D:6%	30	A:11%	B:16%	C:68%	D:5%
13	A:58%	B:21%	C:19%	D:2%	31	A:10%	B:74%	C:5%	D:11%
14	A:32%	B:11%	C:4%	D:53%	32	A:16%	B:21%	C:1%	D:62%
15	A:22%	B:26%	C:39%	D:13%	33	A:16%	B:26%	C:21%	D:37%
16	A:11%	B:20%	C:53%	D:16%	34	A:21%	B:6%	C:68%	D:5%
17	A:16%	B:32%	C:26%	D:26%	35	A:47%	B:18%	C:32%	D:3%
18	A:26%	B:27%	C:21%	D:26%	36	A:1%	B:62%	C:35%	D:2%
19	A:58%	B:26%	C:10%	D:6%	37	A:26%	B:21%	C:32%	D:21%
20	A:1%	B:5%	C:2%	D:92%	38	A:11%	B:25%	C:22%	D:42%
21	A:26%	B:11%	C:58%	D:5%	39	A:26%	B:10%	C:53%	D:11%
22	A:47%	B:48%	C:1%	D:4%	40	A:63%	B:26%	C:5%	D:6%
23	A:37%	B:16%	C:26%	D:21%	41	A:26%	B:21%	C:32%	D:21%
24	A:5%	B:42%	C:37%	D:16%	42	A:11%	B:5%	C:79%	D:5%
25	A:63%	B:16%	C:16%	D:5%	43	A:14%	B:12%	C:33%	D:41%
26	A:32%	B:10%	C:37%	D:21%	44	A:16%	B:21%	C:26%	D:37%

£250,000

#	A	B	C	D	#	A	B	C	D
1	A:47%	B:21%	C:16%	D:16%	21	A:11%	B:5%	C:68%	D:16%
2	A:32%	B:42%	C:22%	D:4%	22	A:26%	B:16%	C:32%	D:26%
3	A:21%	B:31%	C:37%	D:11%	23	A:16%	B:11%	C:68%	D:5%
4	A:2%	B:30%	C:52%	D:16%	24	A:19%	B:74%	C:3%	D:4%
5	A:32%	B:26%	C:26%	D:16%	25	A:53%	B:37%	C:5%	D:5%
6	A:20%	B:32%	C:37%	D:11%	26	A:31%	B:26%	C:1%	D:42%
7	A:16%	B:37%	C:16%	D:31%	27	A:40%	B:54%	C:2%	D:4%
8	A:17%	B:3%	C:79%	D:1%	28	A:47%	B:16%	C:11%	D:26%
9	A:33%	B:15%	C:31%	D:21%	29	A:42%	B:37%	C:16%	D:5%
10	A:16%	B:32%	C:47%	D:5%	30	A:32%	B:62%	C:2%	D:4%
11	A:87%	B:5%	C:1%	D:7%	31	A:92%	B:2%	C:1%	D:5%
12	A:32%	B:42%	C:17%	D:9%	32	A:21%	B:26%	C:37%	D:16%
13	A:72%	B:2%	C:21%	D:5%	33	A:5%	B:16%	C:58%	D:21%
14	A:26%	B:32%	C:16%	D:26%	34	A:72%	B:17%	C:2%	D:9%
15	A:84%	B:1%	C:2%	D:13%	35	A:42%	B:5%	C:37%	D:16%
16	A:37%	B:21%	C:37%	D:5%	36	A:43%	B:37%	C:4%	D:16%
17	A:26%	B:16%	C:47%	D:11%	37	A:26%	B:11%	C:16%	D:47%
18	A:32%	B:31%	C:21%	D:16%	38	A:42%	B:15%	C:21%	D:22%
19	A:10%	B:21%	C:37%	D:32%	39	A:31%	B:12%	C:47%	D:10%
20	A:30%	B:16%	C:53%	D:1%	40	A:53%	B:37%	C:5%	D:5%

ASK THE AUDIENCE

£500,000

#	A	B	C	D	#	A	B	C	D
1	A:16%	B:16%	C:26%	D:42%	19	A:26%	B:26%	C:32%	D:16%
2	A:5%	B:8%	C:84%	D:3%	20	A:21%	B:34%	C:30%	D:15%
3	A:3%	B:26%	C:42%	D:29%	21	A:21%	B:26%	C:47%	D:6%
4	A:32%	B:5%	C:58%	D:5%	22	A:37%	B:2%	C:58%	D:3%
5	A:32%	B:26%	C:32%	D:10%	23	A:21%	B:26%	C:32%	D:21%
6	A:21%	B:63%	C:11%	D:5%	24	A:22%	B:25%	C:42%	D:11%
7	A:49%	B:26%	C:9%	D:16%	25	A:47%	B:16%	C:12%	D:25%
8	A:26%	B:22%	C:47%	D:5%	26	A:83%	B:14%	C:2%	D:1%
9	A:21%	B:21%	C:11%	D:47%	27	A:58%	B:5%	C:11%	D:26%
10	A:32%	B:24%	C:28%	D:16%	28	A:3%	B:47%	C:37%	D:13%
11	A:47%	B:26%	C:21%	D:6%	29	A:21%	B:32%	C:42%	D:5%
12	A:32%	B:57%	C:7%	D:4%	30	A:53%	B:14%	C:21%	D:12%
13	A:32%	B:10%	C:42%	D:16%	31	A:42%	B:16%	C:33%	D:9%
14	A:26%	B:32%	C:29%	D:13%	32	A:47%	B:42%	C:8%	D:3%
15	A:37%	B:16%	C:21%	D:26%	33	A:21%	B:16%	C:10%	D:53%
16	A:58%	B:16%	C:21%	D:5%	34	A:91%	B:2%	C:3%	D:4%
17	A:16%	B:26%	C:35%	D:23%	35	A:16%	B:16%	C:21%	D:47%
18	A:9%	B:2%	C:72%	D:17%	36	A:5%	B:5%	C:6%	D:84%

£1,000,000

#	A	B	C	D	#	A	B	C	D
1	A:37%	B:32%	C:26%	D:5%	17	A:32%	B:59%	C:6%	D:3%
2	A:26%	B:42%	C:11%	D:21%	18	A:53%	B:12%	C:26%	D:9%
3	A:16%	B:26%	C:16%	D:42%	19	A:19%	B:58%	C:8%	D:15%
4	A:26%	B:19%	C:53%	D:2%	20	A:11%	B:15%	C:32%	D:42%
5	A:32%	B:10%	C:26%	D:32%	21	A:21%	B:12%	C:62%	D:5%
6	A:68%	B:16%	C:11%	D:5%	22	A:26%	B:5%	C:53%	D:16%
7	A:5%	B:16%	C:53%	D:26%	23	A:37%	B:37%	C:16%	D:10%
8	A:47%	B:21%	C:29%	D:3%	24	A:22%	B:5%	C:47%	D:26%
9	A:9%	B:34%	C:31%	D:26%	25	A:26%	B:16%	C:47%	D:11%
10	A:12%	B:42%	C:20%	D:26%	26	A:21%	B:37%	C:21%	D:21%
11	A:11%	B:47%	C:26%	D:16%	27	A:26%	B:42%	C:5%	D:27%
12	A:32%	B:16%	C:26%	D:26%	28	A:21%	B:16%	C:37%	D:26%
13	A:26%	B:32%	C:26%	D:16%	29	A:53%	B:32%	C:5%	D:10%
14	A:42%	B:16%	C:16%	D:26%	30	A:47%	B:16%	C:16%	D:21%
15	A:58%	B:5%	C:21%	D:16%	31	A:26%	B:21%	C:42%	D:11%
16	A:16%	B:42%	C:5%	D:37%	32	A:5%	B:63%	C:19%	D:13%

Answers

Fastest Finger First

1	CABD	2	BADC	3	CBAD	4	CADB	5	BDCA
6	CADB	7	BADC	8	ADCB	9	BDAC	10	BDCA
11	CADB	12	DBCA	13	DCBA	14	ACBD	15	CABD
16	BDCA	17	BACD	18	CBAD	19	BDAC	20	BCDA
21	DBAC	22	ADBC	23	BADC	24	BCAD	25	BADC
26	CDBA	27	CDAB	28	BCDA	29	ADBC	30	BACD
31	ACDB	32	CDBA	33	DABC	34	DCAB	35	CABD
36	CBAD	37	BACD	38	CDBA	39	BADC	40	CADB
41	ACDB	42	ACBD	43	BDAC	44	CDBA	45	CDAB
46	BDCA	47	CBAD	48	DACB	49	ACDB	50	DACB
51	ACBD	52	BDCA	53	CBAD	54	DCAB	55	BADC
56	DACB	57	BDAC	58	CABD	59	ACDB	60	DCBA
61	BCDA	62	DCAB	63	CADB	64	ABDC	65	BADC
66	DBCA	67	CABD	68	CBAD	69	BDCA	70	CDAB
71	CBDA	72	CBAD	73	BDCA	74	DCAB	75	CBDA
76	ABDC	77	DCAB	78	DCBA	79	DBAC	80	BCDA
81	DCAB	82	BDAC	83	DABC	84	CDAB	85	BACD
86	BACD	87	DBAC	88	CDBA	89	CADB	90	BADC
91	CADB	92	DACB	93	DBCA	94	DBAC	95	BADC
96	CBDA	97	DBCA	98	BCAD	99	CBDA	100	CBAD

If you answered correctly, well done! Turn to page 31 to play for £100!

£100

1	D	2	D	3	A	4	A	5	C	6	B	7	C
8	B	9	B	10	A	11	A	12	C	13	D	14	A
15	A	16	B	17	C	18	D	19	C	20	A	21	C
22	C	23	B	24	B	25	C	26	C	27	A	28	A
29	A	30	A	31	C	32	C	33	B	34	A	35	C
36	D	37	B	38	D	39	D	40	A	41	D	42	D
43	C	44	B	45	C	46	D	47	B	48	C	49	A
50	A	51	B	52	A	53	D	54	A	55	D	56	C

ANSWERS

57	C	58	A	59	D	60	B	61	B	62	A	63	A
64	D	65	D	66	C	67	C	68	D	69	A	70	B
71	C	72	D	73	B	74	C	75	D	76	B	77	D
78	A	79	C	80	A	81	B	82	C	83	C	84	A
85	C	86	A	87	B	88	C								

If you have won £100, well done! Turn to page 51 to play for £200!

£200

1	A	2	B	3	C	4	A	5	D	6	B	7	D
8	C	9	A	10	C	11	A	12	C	13	B	14	C
15	C	16	B	17	B	18	C	19	A	20	D	21	B
22	D	23	B	24	A	25	B	26	C	27	D	28	C
29	C	30	C	31	A	32	D	33	C	34	A	35	C
36	B	37	C	38	C	39	B	40	A	41	C	42	C
43	A	44	A	45	A	46	B	47	D	48	C	49	B
50	D	51	C	52	D	53	C	54	C	55	B	56	C
57	A	58	C	59	D	60	C	61	C	62	A	63	C
64	B	65	B	66	C	67	A	68	D	69	B	70	A
71	A	72	D	73	A	74	D	75	B	76	C	77	D
78	C	79	A	80	C	81	B	82	D	83	B	84	A

If you have won £200, well done! Turn to page 69 to play for £300!

£300

1	B	2	A	3	D	4	B	5	D	6	B	7	B
8	B	9	C	10	D	11	B	12	C	13	B	14	B
15	A	16	B	17	B	18	A	19	B	20	B	21	D
22	C	23	D	24	C	25	C	26	D	27	B	28	C
29	B	30	B	31	B	32	B	33	C	34	B	35	C
36	C	37	B	38	D	39	C	40	C	41	D	42	B
43	D	44	D	45	B	46	A	47	A	48	C	49	C
50	D	51	D	52	C	53	A	54	A	55	A	56	B
57	D	58	A	59	C	60	B	61	C	62	B	63	B
64	D	65	A	66	C	67	B	68	A	69	A	70	D
71	B	72	C	73	C	74	B	75	A	76	C	77	A
78	D	79	C	80	B									

If you have won £300, well done! Turn to page 87 to play for £500!

ANSWERS

£500

1	B	2	C	3	A	4	D	5	A	6	D	7	A
8	D	9	C	10	D	11	B	12	A	13	B	14	B
15	A	16	C	17	D	18	B	19	B	20	A	21	D
22	C	23	C	24	A	25	B	26	D	27	B	28	C
29	B	30	C	31	B	32	C	33	D	34	C	35	B
36	D	37	B	38	A	39	C	40	A	41	B	42	D
43	C	44	A	45	C	46	D	47	D	48	D	49	D
50	C	51	B	52	D	53	D	54	A	55	D	56	A
57	B	58	B	59	C	60	D	61	D	62	B	63	B
64	B	65	A	66	A	67	B	68	D	69	B	70	C
71	A	72	A	73	D	74	C	75	D	76	D		

If you have won £500, well done! Turn to page 105 to play for £1,000!

£1,000

1	D	2	B	3	C	4	A	5	B	6	D	7	C
8	B	9	C	10	C	11	B	12	B	13	D	14	B
15	B	16	B	17	A	18	D	19	B	20	D	21	B
22	B	23	A	24	A	25	C	26	A	27	D	28	B
29	B	30	B	31	C	32	D	33	B	34	D	35	C
36	D	37	C	38	C	39	C	40	C	41	B	42	C
43	C	44	A	45	B	46	D	47	C	48	B	49	B
50	C	51	C	52	B	53	D	54	B	55	D	56	B
57	D	58	C	59	C	60	A	61	D	62	C	63	B
64	A	65	C	66	B	67	B	68	C	69	D	70	A
71	D	72	B										

If you have won £1,000, well done! Turn to page 121 to play for £2,000!

£2,000

1	B	2	A	3	B	4	A	5	B	6	A	7	A
8	C	9	A	10	A	11	B	12	D	13	A	14	B
15	D	16	D	17	B	18	B	19	C	20	D	21	B
22	D	23	C	24	B	25	D	26	C	27	A	28	C
29	C	30	D	31	A	32	A	33	B	34	B	35	B
36	D	37	C	38	A	39	A	40	C	41	D	42	B
43	A	44	C	45	D	46	B	47	C	48	B	49	A
50	A	51	C	52	B	53	A	54	C	55	B	56	B
57	C	58	B	59	B	60	C	61	B	62	B	63	A
64	C	65	C	66	B	67	C	68	B				

If you have won £2,000, well done! Turn to page 137 to play for £4,000!

ANSWERS

£4,000

1	B	2	A	3	A	4	A	5	C	6	A	7	A
8	C	9	A	10	A	11	D	12	D	13	C	14	D
15	C	16	A	17	A	18	A	19	B	20	A	21	C
22	A	23	A	24	C	25	B	26	A	27	D	28	C
29	C	30	B	31	D	32	A	33	D	34	C	35	C
36	C	37	D	38	A	39	A	40	B	41	C	42	A
43	C	44	B	45	B	46	A	47	A	48	A	49	C
50	C	51	A	52	C	53	A	54	B	55	A	56	C
57	A	58	C	59	B	60	C	61	C	62	D	63	A
64	C												

If you have won £4,000, well done! Turn to page 151 to play for £8,000!

£8,000

1	C	2	B	3	A	4	B	5	A	6	B	7	D
8	C	9	C	10	B	11	A	12	C	13	C	14	B
15	B	16	B	17	D	18	B	19	C	20	B	21	B
22	C	23	D	24	C	25	B	26	A	27	B	28	D
29	B	30	B	31	C	32	B	33	A	34	B	35	B
36	C	37	A	38	B	39	C	40	B	41	C	42	D
43	C	44	A	45	D	46	B	47	C	48	B	49	C
50	D	51	A	52	B	53	A	54	B	55	A	56	B
57	B	58	B	59	C	60	A						

If you have won £8,000, well done! Turn to page 165 to play for £16,000!

£16,000

1	C	2	A	3	B	4	A	5	B	6	A	7	C
8	D	9	A	10	C	11	B	12	C	13	C	14	B
15	B	16	C	17	D	18	D	19	C	20	B	21	A
22	C	23	A	24	B	25	A	26	C	27	A	28	C
29	D	30	D	31	D	32	C	33	C	34	C	35	B
36	A	37	D	38	C	39	A	40	B	41	C	42	B
43	C	44	B	45	B	46	A	47	B	48	B	49	B
50	B	51	D	52	C	53	A	54	D	55	A	56	C

If you have won £16,000, well done! Turn to page 179 to play for £32,000!

ANSWERS

£32,000

1	D	2	C	3	C	4	A	5	A	6	A	7	A
8	B	9	B	10	C	11	A	12	A	13	A	14	A
15	D	16	A	17	B	18	B	19	D	20	A	21	A
22	B	23	B	24	D	25	C	26	A	27	B	28	B
29	B	30	B	31	B	32	A	33	B	34	B	35	B
36	B	37	B	38	D	39	B	40	B	41	B	42	A
43	D	44	B	45	C	46	A	47	D	48	C	49	B
50	C	51	C	52	D								

If you have won £32,000, well done! Turn to page 191 to play for £64,000!

£64,000

1	B	2	B	3	C	4	A	5	A	6	C	7	C
8	A	9	C	10	C	11	C	12	B	13	B	14	C
15	B	16	A	17	D	18	D	19	B	20	B	21	B
22	B	23	D	24	B	25	D	26	C	27	C	28	D
29	C	30	D	31	B	32	B	33	A	34	D	35	C
36	B	37	A	38	B	39	B	40	B	41	A	42	C
43	A	44	A	45	B	46	C	47	B	48	A		

If you have won £64,000, well done! Turn to page 203 to play for £125,000!

£125,000

1	C	2	A	3	C	4	B	5	C	6	B	7	B
8	C	9	C	10	D	11	B	12	B	13	A	14	D
15	C	16	B	17	D	18	A	19	A	20	D	21	B
22	A	23	A	24	B	25	A	26	C	27	B	28	B
29	C	30	C	31	B	32	D	33	D	34	C	35	C
36	B	37	C	38	B	39	A	40	B	41	C	42	C
43	C	44	C										

If you have won £125,000, well done! Turn to page 213 to play for £250,000!

£250,000

1	B	2	C	3	C	4	C	5	B	6	A	7	B
8	C	9	C	10	B	11	A	12	B	13	A	14	C
15	A	16	C	17	C	18	A	19	D	20	C	21	C
22	B	23	C	24	B	25	B	26	D	27	A	28	A
29	B	30	B	31	A	32	A	33	C	34	A	35	A
36	B	37	D	38	A	39	C	40	D				

If you have won £250,000, well done! Turn to page 223 to play for £500,000!

ANSWERS

£500,000

1	B	2	C	3	C	4	C	5	B	6	B	7	A
8	A	9	A	10	C	11	D	12	A	13	B	14	C
15	A	16	A	17	C	18	C	19	A	20	C	21	C
22	C	23	A	24	C	25	A	26	A	27	A	28	B
29	C	30	A	31	A	32	B	33	D	34	A	35	D
36	D												

If you have won £500,000, well done! Turn to page 233 to play for £1,000,000!

£1,000,000

1	B	2	A	3	D	4	C	5	D	6	A	7	C
8	B	9	B	10	D	11	D	12	C	13	A	14	D
15	A	16	C	17	B	18	A	19	B	20	C	21	C
22	C	23	A	24	C	25	C	26	D	27	B	28	D
29	A	30	A	31	C	32	B								

If you have won £1,000,000, well done! You're a millionaire!

Score sheets

Write your name and the names of any other contestants in the space provided. Shade in each of the boxes lightly with a pencil once you or one of your fellow contestants has won the amount in that box. If you or any of the other contestants answer a question incorrectly and are out of the game, use a soft eraser to rub out the relevant boxes so that the final score is showing.

SCORE SHEET

contestant's name	contestant's name
....	....

50:50	☎	👥		50:50	☎	👥
☐	☐	☐		☐	☐	☐

15	£1 MILLION	15	£1 MILLION
14	£500,000	14	£500,000
13	£250,000	13	£250,000
12	£125,000	12	£125,000
11	£64,000	11	£64,000
10	£32,000	**10**	£32,000
9	£16,000	9	£16,000
8	£8,000	8	£8,000
7	£4,000	7	£4,000
6	£2,000	6	£2,000
5	£1,000	**5**	£1,000
4	£500	4	£500
3	£300	3	£300
2	£200	2	£200
1	£100	1	£100

SCORE SHEET

contestant's name	contestant's name
....	....

50:50	☎	👥		50:50	☎	👥
☐	☐	☐		☐	☐	☐

15	£1 MILLION		15	£1 MILLION
14	£500,000		14	£500,000
13	£250,000		13	£250,000
12	£125,000		12	£125,000
11	£64,000		11	£64,000
10	£32,000		10	£32,000
9	£16,000		9	£16,000
8	£8,000		8	£8,000
7	£4,000		7	£4,000
6	£2,000		6	£2,000
5	£1,000		5	£1,000
4	£500		4	£500
3	£300		3	£300
2	£200		2	£200
1	£100		1	£100

SCORE SHEET

contestant's name	contestant's name
....	....

50:50	☎	👥	50:50	☎	👥
☐	☐	☐	☐	☐	☐

15	£1 MILLION	15	£1 MILLION
14	£500,000	14	£500,000
13	£250,000	13	£250,000
12	£125,000	12	£125,000
11	£64,000	11	£64,000
10	£32,000	**10**	£32,000
9	£16,000	9	£16,000
8	£8,000	8	£8,000
7	£4,000	7	£4,000
6	£2,000	6	£2,000
5	£1,000	**5**	£1,000
4	£500	4	£500
3	£300	3	£300
2	£200	2	£200
1	£100	1	£100

SCORE SHEET

contestant's name

....

50:50 ☎ 👥

☐ ☐ ☐

15	£1 MILLION
14	£500,000
13	£250,000
12	£125,000
11	£64,000
10	£32,000
9	£16,000
8	£8,000
7	£4,000
6	£2,000
5	£1,000
4	£500
3	£300
2	£200
1	£100

contestant's name

....

50:50 ☎ 👥

☐ ☐ ☐

15	£1 MILLION
14	£500,000
13	£250,000
12	£125,000
11	£64,000
10	£32,000
9	£16,000
8	£8,000
7	£4,000
6	£2,000
5	£1,000
4	£500
3	£300
2	£200
1	£100

SCORE SHEET

contestant's name	contestant's name
....	....
50:50 📞 👥	50:50 📞 👥
☐ ☐ ☐	☐ ☐ ☐

15	£1 MILLION	15	£1 MILLION
14	£500,000	14	£500,000
13	£250,000	13	£250,000
12	£125,000	12	£125,000
11	£64,000	11	£64,000
10	£32,000	10	£32,000
9	£16,000	9	£16,000
8	£8,000	8	£8,000
7	£4,000	7	£4,000
6	£2,000	6	£2,000
5	£1,000	5	£1,000
4	£500	4	£500
3	£300	3	£300
2	£200	2	£200
1	£100	1	£100

SCORE SHEET

contestant's name	contestant's name
....	....

50:50	☎	👥👥		50:50	☎	👥👥
☐	☐	☐		☐	☐	☐

15	£1 MILLION	15	£1 MILLION
14	£500,000	14	£500,000
13	£250,000	13	£250,000
12	£125,000	12	£125,000
11	£64,000	11	£64,000
10	£32,000	10	£32,000
9	£16,000	9	£16,000
8	£8,000	8	£8,000
7	£4,000	7	£4,000
6	£2,000	6	£2,000
5	£1,000	5	£1,000
4	£500	4	£500
3	£300	3	£300
2	£200	2	£200
1	£100	1	£100

S C O R E   S H E E T

contestant's name	contestant's name
....	....

50:50	☎	👥		50:50	☎	👥
☐	☐	☐		☐	☐	☐

15	£1 MILLION		15	£1 MILLION
14	£500,000		14	£500,000
13	£250,000		13	£250,000
12	£125,000		12	£125,000
11	£64,000		11	£64,000
10	£32,000		**10**	£32,000
9	£16,000		9	£16,000
8	£8,000		8	£8,000
7	£4,000		7	£4,000
6	£2,000		6	£2,000
5	£1,000		**5**	£1,000
4	£500		4	£500
3	£300		3	£300
2	£200		2	£200
1	£100		1	£100

SCORE SHEET

contestant's name	contestant's name
....	....

50:50	⚡📞	👥👤👥	50:50	⚡📞	👥👤👥
☐	☐	☐	☐	☐	☐

15	£1 MILLION	15	£1 MILLION
14	£500,000	14	£500,000
13	£250,000	13	£250,000
12	£125,000	12	£125,000
11	£64,000	11	£64,000
10	£32,000	**10**	£32,000
9	£16,000	9	£16,000
8	£8,000	8	£8,000
7	£4,000	7	£4,000
6	£2,000	6	£2,000
5	£1,000	**5**	£1,000
4	£500	4	£500
3	£300	3	£300
2	£200	2	£200
1	£100	1	£100

SCORE SHEET

contestant's name	contestant's name
....	....

50:50 ☎ 👥	50:50 ☎ 👥
☐ ☐ ☐	☐ ☐ ☐

15	£1 MILLION	15	£1 MILLION
14	£500,000	14	£500,000
13	£250,000	13	£250,000
12	£125,000	12	£125,000
11	£64,000	11	£64,000
10	£32,000	**10**	£32,000
9	£16,000	9	£16,000
8	£8,000	8	£8,000
7	£4,000	7	£4,000
6	£2,000	6	£2,000
5	£1,000	**5**	£1,000
4	£500	4	£500
3	£300	3	£300
2	£200	2	£200
1	£100	1	£100

SCORE SHEET

contestant's name

....

50:50 ☎ 👥

☐ ☐ ☐

15	£1 MILLION
14	£500,000
13	£250,000
12	£125,000
11	£64,000
10	£32,000
9	£16,000
8	£8,000
7	£4,000
6	£2,000
5	£1,000
4	£500
3	£300
2	£200
1	£100

contestant's name

....

50:50 ☎ 👥

☐ ☐ ☐

15	£1 MILLION
14	£500,000
13	£250,000
12	£125,000
11	£64,000
10	£32,000
9	£16,000
8	£8,000
7	£4,000
6	£2,000
5	£1,000
4	£500
3	£300
2	£200
1	£100

SCORE SHEET

contestant's name

....

50:50 · · ·

☐ ☐ ☐

contestant's name

....

50:50 · · ·

☐ ☐ ☐

15	£1 MILLION
14	£500,000
13	£250,000
12	£125,000
11	£64,000
10	£32,000
9	£16,000
8	£8,000
7	£4,000
6	£2,000
5	£1,000
4	£500
3	£300
2	£200
1	£100

15	£1 MILLION
14	£500,000
13	£250,000
12	£125,000
11	£64,000
10	£32,000
9	£16,000
8	£8,000
7	£4,000
6	£2,000
5	£1,000
4	£500
3	£300
2	£200
1	£100

SCORE SHEET

contestant's name	contestant's name
....	....

50:50			50:50		
☐	☐	☐	☐	☐	☐

15	£1 MILLION	15	£1 MILLION
14	£500,000	14	£500,000
13	£250,000	13	£250,000
12	£125,000	12	£125,000
11	£64,000	11	£64,000
10	£32,000	10	£32,000
9	£16,000	9	£16,000
8	£8,000	8	£8,000
7	£4,000	7	£4,000
6	£2,000	6	£2,000
5	£1,000	5	£1,000
4	£500	4	£500
3	£300	3	£300
2	£200	2	£200
1	£100	1	£100

SCORE SHEET

contestant's name

....

contestant's name

....

50:50	☎	👥
☐	☐	☐

50:50	☎	👥
☐	☐	☐

15	£1 MILLION		15	£1 MILLION
14	£500,000		14	£500,000
13	£250,000		13	£250,000
12	£125,000		12	£125,000
11	£64,000		11	£64,000
10	£32,000		**10**	£32,000
9	£16,000		9	£16,000
8	£8,000		8	£8,000
7	£4,000		7	£4,000
6	£2,000		6	£2,000
5	£1,000		**5**	£1,000
4	£500		4	£500
3	£300		3	£300
2	£200		2	£200
1	£100		1	£100

SCORE SHEET

contestant's name		contestant's name	
....		....	

50:50 ☎ 👥 □ □ □   50:50 ☎ 👥 □ □ □

15	£1 MILLION	15	£1 MILLION
14	£500,000	14	£500,000
13	£250,000	13	£250,000
12	£125,000	12	£125,000
11	£64,000	11	£64,000
10	£32,000	10	£32,000
9	£16,000	9	£16,000
8	£8,000	8	£8,000
7	£4,000	7	£4,000
6	£2,000	6	£2,000
5	£1,000	5	£1,000
4	£500	4	£500
3	£300	3	£300
2	£200	2	£200
1	£100	1	£100

SCORE SHEET

contestant's name

....

50:50

15	£1 MILLION
14	£500,000
13	£250,000
12	£125,000
11	£64,000
10	£32,000
9	£16,000
8	£8,000
7	£4,000
6	£2,000
5	£1,000
4	£500
3	£300
2	£200
1	£100

contestant's name

....

50:50

15	£1 MILLION
14	£500,000
13	£250,000
12	£125,000
11	£64,000
10	£32,000
9	£16,000
8	£8,000
7	£4,000
6	£2,000
5	£1,000
4	£500
3	£300
2	£200
1	£100

SCORE SHEET

contestant's name

....

50:50

15	£1 MILLION
14	£500,000
13	£250,000
12	£125,000
11	£64,000
10	£32,000
9	£16,000
8	£8,000
7	£4,000
6	£2,000
5	£1,000
4	£500
3	£300
2	£200
1	£100

contestant's name

....

50:50

15	£1 MILLION
14	£500,000
13	£250,000
12	£125,000
11	£64,000
10	£32,000
9	£16,000
8	£8,000
7	£4,000
6	£2,000
5	£1,000
4	£500
3	£300
2	£200
1	£100

SCORE SHEET

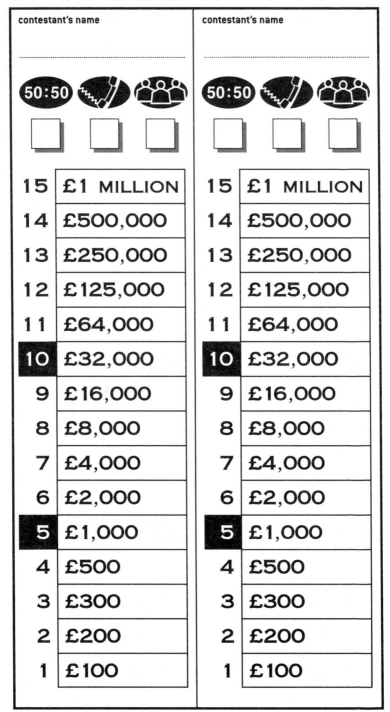

contestant's name	contestant's name
....	....

50:50	☎	👥	50:50	☎	👥	
☐	☐	☐	☐	☐	☐	

15	£1 MILLION	15	£1 MILLION
14	£500,000	14	£500,000
13	£250,000	13	£250,000
12	£125,000	12	£125,000
11	£64,000	11	£64,000
10	£32,000	**10**	£32,000
9	£16,000	9	£16,000
8	£8,000	8	£8,000
7	£4,000	7	£4,000
6	£2,000	6	£2,000
5	£1,000	**5**	£1,000
4	£500	4	£500
3	£300	3	£300
2	£200	2	£200
1	£100	1	£100

SCORE SHEET

contestant's name

....

50:50

contestant's name

....

50:50

15	£1 MILLION	15	£1 MILLION
14	£500,000	14	£500,000
13	£250,000	13	£250,000
12	£125,000	12	£125,000
11	£64,000	11	£64,000
10	£32,000	10	£32,000
9	£16,000	9	£16,000
8	£8,000	8	£8,000
7	£4,000	7	£4,000
6	£2,000	6	£2,000
5	£1,000	5	£1,000
4	£500	4	£500
3	£300	3	£300
2	£200	2	£200
1	£100	1	£100

SCORE SHEET

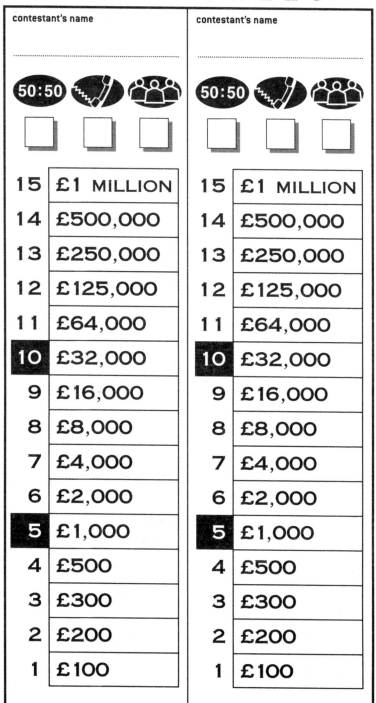

contestant's name	contestant's name
....	....

15	£1 MILLION	15	£1 MILLION
14	£500,000	14	£500,000
13	£250,000	13	£250,000
12	£125,000	12	£125,000
11	£64,000	11	£64,000
10	£32,000	10	£32,000
9	£16,000	9	£16,000
8	£8,000	8	£8,000
7	£4,000	7	£4,000
6	£2,000	6	£2,000
5	£1,000	5	£1,000
4	£500	4	£500
3	£300	3	£300
2	£200	2	£200
1	£100	1	£100

SCORE SHEET

contestant's name	contestant's name
....	....

50:50 ⚡ 👥☐ ☐ ☐   50:50 ⚡ 👥☐ ☐ ☐

15	£1 MILLION	15	£1 MILLION
14	£500,000	14	£500,000
13	£250,000	13	£250,000
12	£125,000	12	£125,000
11	£64,000	11	£64,000
10	£32,000	**10**	£32,000
9	£16,000	9	£16,000
8	£8,000	8	£8,000
7	£4,000	7	£4,000
6	£2,000	6	£2,000
5	£1,000	**5**	£1,000
4	£500	4	£500
3	£300	3	£300
2	£200	2	£200
1	£100	1	£100

SCORE SHEET

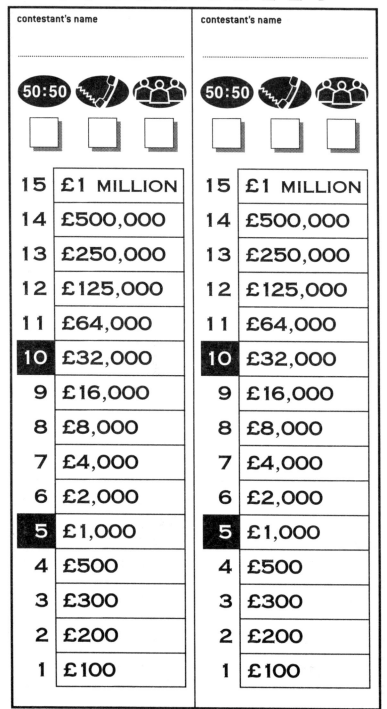

contestant's name		contestant's name	
....		....	
50:50 📞 👥		50:50 📞 👥	
☐ ☐ ☐		☐ ☐ ☐	
15	£1 MILLION	15	£1 MILLION
14	£500,000	14	£500,000
13	£250,000	13	£250,000
12	£125,000	12	£125,000
11	£64,000	11	£64,000
10	£32,000	10	£32,000
9	£16,000	9	£16,000
8	£8,000	8	£8,000
7	£4,000	7	£4,000
6	£2,000	6	£2,000
5	£1,000	5	£1,000
4	£500	4	£500
3	£300	3	£300
2	£200	2	£200
1	£100	1	£100

SCORE SHEET

contestant's name	contestant's name
....	....

50:50	☎	👥	50:50	☎	👥
☐	☐	☐	☐	☐	☐

15	£1 MILLION	15	£1 MILLION
14	£500,000	14	£500,000
13	£250,000	13	£250,000
12	£125,000	12	£125,000
11	£64,000	11	£64,000
10	£32,000	**10**	£32,000
9	£16,000	9	£16,000
8	£8,000	8	£8,000
7	£4,000	7	£4,000
6	£2,000	6	£2,000
5	£1,000	**5**	£1,000
4	£500	4	£500
3	£300	3	£300
2	£200	2	£200
1	£100	1	£100

SCORE SHEET

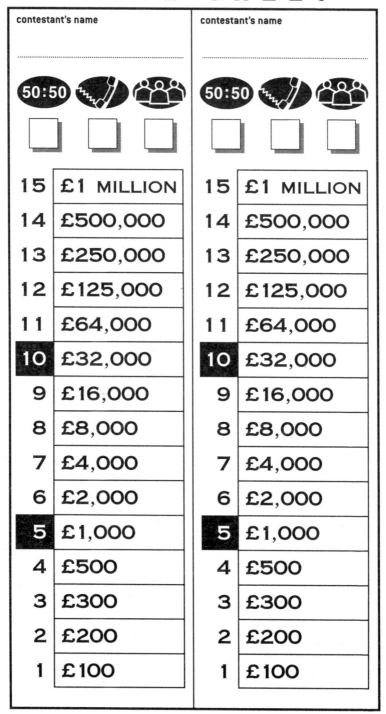

contestant's name	contestant's name
....	....

15	£1 MILLION	
14	£500,000	
13	£250,000	
12	£125,000	
11	£64,000	
10	£32,000	
9	£16,000	
8	£8,000	
7	£4,000	
6	£2,000	
5	£1,000	
4	£500	
3	£300	
2	£200	
1	£100	

15	£1 MILLION
14	£500,000
13	£250,000
12	£125,000
11	£64,000
10	£32,000
9	£16,000
8	£8,000
7	£4,000
6	£2,000
5	£1,000
4	£500
3	£300
2	£200
1	£100

SCORE SHEET

contestant's name	contestant's name
....	....

50:50	☎	👥	50:50	☎	👥
☐	☐	☐	☐	☐	☐

15	£1 MILLION	15	£1 MILLION
14	£500,000	14	£500,000
13	£250,000	13	£250,000
12	£125,000	12	£125,000
11	£64,000	11	£64,000
10	£32,000	**10**	£32,000
9	£16,000	9	£16,000
8	£8,000	8	£8,000
7	£4,000	7	£4,000
6	£2,000	6	£2,000
5	£1,000	**5**	£1,000
4	£500	4	£500
3	£300	3	£300
2	£200	2	£200
1	£100	1	£100

SCORE SHEET

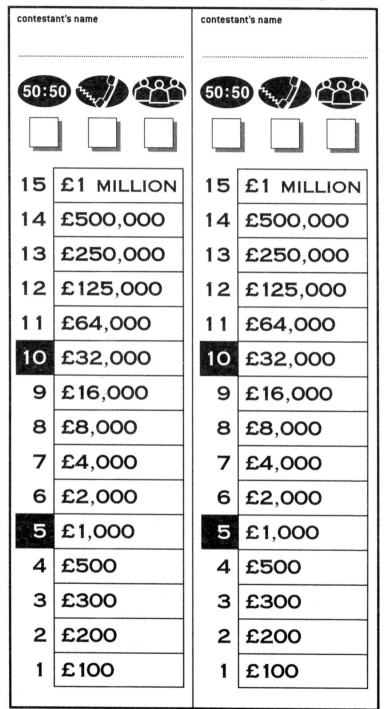

contestant's name	contestant's name
50:50 📞 👥 ☐ ☐ ☐	50:50 📞 👥 ☐ ☐ ☐

15	£1 MILLION	15	£1 MILLION
14	£500,000	14	£500,000
13	£250,000	13	£250,000
12	£125,000	12	£125,000
11	£64,000	11	£64,000
10	£32,000	10	£32,000
9	£16,000	9	£16,000
8	£8,000	8	£8,000
7	£4,000	7	£4,000
6	£2,000	6	£2,000
5	£1,000	5	£1,000
4	£500	4	£500
3	£300	3	£300
2	£200	2	£200
1	£100	1	£100

S C O R E S H E E T

contestant's name	contestant's name
....	....

50:50	☎	👥👥👥		50:50	☎	👥👥👥
☐	☐	☐		☐	☐	☐

15	£1 MILLION		15	£1 MILLION
14	£500,000		14	£500,000
13	£250,000		13	£250,000
12	£125,000		12	£125,000
11	£64,000		11	£64,000
10	£32,000		**10**	£32,000
9	£16,000		9	£16,000
8	£8,000		8	£8,000
7	£4,000		7	£4,000
6	£2,000		6	£2,000
5	£1,000		**5**	£1,000
4	£500		4	£500
3	£300		3	£300
2	£200		2	£200
1	£100		1	£100

S C O R E   S H E E T

contestant's name	contestant's name
....	....

50:50	☎	👥		50:50	☎	👥
☐	☐	☐		☐	☐	☐

15	£1 MILLION	15	£1 MILLION
14	£500,000	14	£500,000
13	£250,000	13	£250,000
12	£125,000	12	£125,000
11	£64,000	11	£64,000
10	£32,000	10	£32,000
9	£16,000	9	£16,000
8	£8,000	8	£8,000
7	£4,000	7	£4,000
6	£2,000	6	£2,000
5	£1,000	5	£1,000
4	£500	4	£500
3	£300	3	£300
2	£200	2	£200
1	£100	1	£100

S C O R E   S H E E T

contestant's name	contestant's name
....	....

50:50			50:50		
☐	☐	☐	☐	☐	☐

15	£1 MILLION	15	£1 MILLION
14	£500,000	14	£500,000
13	£250,000	13	£250,000
12	£125,000	12	£125,000
11	£64,000	11	£64,000
10	£32,000	**10**	£32,000
9	£16,000	9	£16,000
8	£8,000	8	£8,000
7	£4,000	7	£4,000
6	£2,000	6	£2,000
5	£1,000	**5**	£1,000
4	£500	4	£500
3	£300	3	£300
2	£200	2	£200
1	£100	1	£100

SCORE SHEET

contestant's name		contestant's name	
....		....	

50:50 📞 👥 □ □ □   **50:50** 📞 👥 □ □ □

15	£1 MILLION	15	£1 MILLION
14	£500,000	14	£500,000
13	£250,000	13	£250,000
12	£125,000	12	£125,000
11	£64,000	11	£64,000
10	£32,000	**10**	£32,000
9	£16,000	9	£16,000
8	£8,000	8	£8,000
7	£4,000	7	£4,000
6	£2,000	6	£2,000
5	£1,000	**5**	£1,000
4	£500	4	£500
3	£300	3	£300
2	£200	2	£200
1	£100	1	£100

SCORE SHEET

contestant's name	contestant's name
....	....

50:50	☎	👥		50:50	☎	👥
☐	☐	☐		☐	☐	☐

15	£1 MILLION		15	£1 MILLION
14	£500,000		14	£500,000
13	£250,000		13	£250,000
12	£125,000		12	£125,000
11	£64,000		11	£64,000
10	£32,000		10	£32,000
9	£16,000		9	£16,000
8	£8,000		8	£8,000
7	£4,000		7	£4,000
6	£2,000		6	£2,000
5	£1,000		5	£1,000
4	£500		4	£500
3	£300		3	£300
2	£200		2	£200
1	£100		1	£100

WHO WANTS TO BE A
MILLIONAIRE?
JUNIOR QUIZ BOOK

The 1st edition Junior Quiz Book has 1000 tormenting questions written for you by the cleverest people in TV – the *Who Wants To Be A Millionaire?* question masters. So be prepared for some serious brain ache as you work your way through this easy to play format. Complete with Fastest Finger First and all 3 Lifelines.

ISBN 0 7522 19642   £5.99

Available from all good bookshops or order direct from
Book Post
PO Box 29
Douglas
Isle of Man
IM99 1BQ

Telephone: 01624 675137   Fax: 01624 670932
E-mail: bookshop@enterprise.net